ANDREW STADTMAUER

The Code

The Purpose of Life and How to Achieve it

S P

To my darling wife and four precious children. You are my everything.

"Those who have a 'why' to live, can bear with almost any 'how'."

Viktor E. Frankl, Man's Search for Meaning

Contents

II   The Path

III   The System

IV   Proposals on the Individual

Preface

Man has sought after many things. Aristotle sought wisdom while St. Aquinas sought God. Schopenhauer sought an escape from striving while Nietzsche sought for power. What is it that I seek? Simply the good of my family and by extension that of the world.
Anonymous

This book sets out to answer the vital questions that we all face, such as the meaning of life, how we should act, and the things that truly matter. If you are like me, then these are prescient questions that need answers if we are to seek after and live a happy and fulfilling life. The great news is that you already know the answers to these questions, they are as innate and natural as breathing. As we journey together, we will approach these questions in turn, firstly examining the questions and then step by step showing the self-evident truth of the answers.

I wrote this book because I was looking for answers and clarity in my life after suffering an irreconcilable loss of faith in and consequently abandoning Christianity. For me, it was a way of organising and clarifying my thoughts as I worked my way to a new moral system and discovered what I believe to be the true purpose of life. In the process, I found happiness, purpose, and peace. I offer it to you in the hope that you will find the same.

This work consists of three parts that are broken into six books. Part one consists of book one alone, which explains the impulse for this work and endeavours to set out the philosophical and metaphysical basis for the system developed in this work. In this book, we discover the purpose of life and how it relates to us. The reader who is not familiar with or uninterested in the more esoteric elements of philosophy may be best served in skipping chapters two, three, and four to begin with. If you are so inclined, leave these relatively dense chapters until such a time when their arcane logic may appeal and allow yourself the freedom to move forward.

Books two and three build on the philosophical foundations of the first book, examining how we can achieve our purpose as human beings. In book two, we define the key terms which are essential to the understanding of this work, examining the nature of the self, the family and the community, and defining, in general terms, our duties to each. Book three takes these duties and codifies them systematically. In this book, we familiarise ourselves with the hierarchy of duty, prioritisation, morality, and finally, present the 'framework for moral decision-making'. Books four and five infer from the system developed in the previous books to create a practical guide for life. They explore some of the outcomes of putting the moral system described in the earlier chapters into place and discussing the character and virtues that are necessary to develop if we are to achieve the purpose we aim for. Book six ends this work, offering the reader a straightforward path to achieving the purpose we strive for and explaining how this path leads to happiness.

This work is the outcome of many hours of reading, discussion, and reflection and is, to the best of my ability, the truth as I understand it to be. As you read this book, take the time to pause and truly consider both what it is that I am suggesting, and the implications that follow from those suggestions. I will have succeeded in my aim in sharing this work only if you, the reader, are prompted to careful contemplation by it. I do not seek your agreement, only your consideration, and if you are so disposed, your reasoned critique.

I

The Logic

1

Origins

So, where do we begin? Like many of you, I grew up in a Christian home. I was introduced to Christianity at an early age, and in many ways, the Christian worldview was conceptually similar to gravity or any of the other absolutes of reality. Simply put, the existence of the Christian God was an immutable fact. Where there were conflicts between my natural impulses and that of the scriptures, I justified them to myself at the moment and repented later. I never considered that perhaps the fault lied in the fundamental nature of the religion, not with me. This settlement changed just before I turned thirty. My oldest son had just reached an age where, like all children, he was curious about everything. One day, he asked me, "Dad, what happens when we die?"

I responded with the standard Christian response; "When you die, if you have been good, you go to heaven, and if you have been evil, you go to hell." Over the next few weeks, I began to wonder for the first time in years whether this was 100% correct. I began to investigate what the scriptures and the theologians thought and said. To my surprise, there was a great deal of confusion amongst the faithful as to exactly what happened after death. I began to wonder, if the most attractive element of Christianity is in doubt, then what else in my faith was up for debate?

Finally, I decided that the only logical thing to do was to start at the beginning and work my way forward. I expected that this would be a process that would reaffirm my faith. Instead, it destroyed it. I began quite naturally enough with Genesis. I was confident that this would hold no particular challenge to my faith as, to me, Thomas Aquinas's five ways seemingly answered all comers. Each iteration of scientific genesis theory merely acting to move the act of creation further back in time relative to ourselves and unfolding creation in ever greater complexity and magnificence. Unfortunately for my faith, I did not even get to the creation of the universe. I stumbled at the first hurdle, so to speak.

As I read and considered that God had created the angels and that Satan had rebelled with a third of the angels, leading to a war in heaven and his final exile to earth, I began to have severe doubts. How and why would anyone rebel against an omnipotent and omniscient being, especially if he was om-nibenevolent? More importantly, I was struck by the paradox of a being of unlimited power, sending his servants to fight his battles on his behalf. Wouldn't God, if he were all-powerful, all-knowing, and all good, find some way to correct his servant's mistakes while avoiding harming or allowing harm to come to his other servants?

Next, I wondered about our world. As a Christian, I had been told that we were Christ's soldiers fighting Satan and his demons in our world. Yet how could this be? Had we not been assured that Jesus had 'broken the power of the devil' after his crucifixion? Why did we need to fight if our God was genuinely omnipotent and omniscient? Couldn't he just end the war whenever he wanted?

Maybe there was no devil at all, I thought. Perhaps it was just us using our freedom to follow our desires. Harming others and doing evil as a result. Without a devil to blame for those desires or tempting man, those desires fall at God's feet.

These questions opened up Pandora's box. I had wondered on to the problem of natural evil. Why, if God was omnibenevolent, was there such a thing as natural evil (natural disasters, diseases, parasites, congenital disabilities, etc.)? Why did humans and animals share similar basic desires? On the surface, none of these things were caused by our free will, they were simply part of the design or nature of reality. Furthermore, there did not seem to be any discrimination between the faithful and non-believers in the distribution of natural evil. Righteous and unrighteous alike suffered, a point driven home in even greater detail by the horrific accounts of nineteenth-century missionaries in Africa.

As I considered the '*theodicies*' for this the problem of natural evil, I found them wanting. The Augustine defence 'that natural evil exists as a punishment for our original sin' seemed to be contra to the supposed omnibenevolence of God. Hick's soul-making theodicy, which stated that 'suffering is natural and as a consequence of free will was necessary so that we could develop from morally immature creatures to morally perfected ones' also seemed wanting. After all, suffering was hardly evenly distributed. It was a universally observed fact, constant throughout time, that the wicked often prospered while the righteous suffered. Gottfried Leibniz's best of all possible worlds, Theodicy, which stated that '*God knowing all possible universes, being limited to the creation of one, being determined to create and being good would result in the creation of the best possible universe*' left me flat. After all, for this theodicy to be true, God would be limited by something and, therefore, could not be omnipotent.

As I considered these challenges to my faith, I realised that there were four possibilities. One, God simply lacked the power to destroy the devil or create a better world without natural evil, namely that he was not omnipotent. Two, God, while having the power to destroy the devil or create a better world, chose not to. By this choice, God chose to allow suffering and evil, which could have been avoided. These outcomes would lead to the conclusion that he was not omnibenevolent. Three, God was both omnipotent and omnibenevolent but was unaware of the world's evil. Or four, a combination of the three. I realised that any of these four possibilities would lead to the inexorable conclusion that the God described in the Judo-Christian tradition could not exist as described.

This realisation was momentous, and after a period of soul-searching, I abandoned my faith and begun my search for the truth. It is this journey that I invite you to join me on. Like René Descartes, we need to start by demolishing every one of our beliefs and beginning as it were with a clean slate. Questioning everything, we have held to be right or wrong and opening ourselves with a willingness to bound ourselves faithfully to the truths we find, and those duties become apparent on our journey. However, before we can begin, we need to set out some rules, some measures to hold ourselves to lest we become lost in contradiction and paradox.

To this end, I proposed to myself and I suggest, in turn, to you that we set our rules as follows. One, any principle must flow logically from a previous principle or a self-evident truth, and two, no principle can contradict any other principle. With these rules, I began once again at the beginning of everything with the metaphysics of existence.

2

Metaphysics

"Thus we see, on the one hand, the existence of the whole world necessarily dependent upon the first conscious being, however undeveloped it may be; on the other hand, this conscious being just as necessarily entirely dependent upon a long chain of causes and effects which have preceded it, and in which it itself appears as a small link."

Authur Schopenhauer, The World as Will and Idea

Metaphysics is a broad field in philosophy, though, in this work, we shall limit ourselves to understanding it to mean the nature of our perceived reality. As we are starting from nothing so to speak, it is natural to begin by asking what the nature of the reality in which we exist is. Do not worry I'm not going to lead you into a morass of monads and existential paradoxes such as if we can know anything and what is reality. Instead, we are going to agree as a starting point to some basics, which

I hope you will agree are self-evident truths. These are that we know "a priori" or before experience that we exist. This logical starting point can be validated by the famous revelation by René Descarte (and for that matter Aristotle) "Cogito, ergo sum" or I think therefore I am. I ask you to accept this as a self-evident and assumed truth. This truth is essential as if we do not exist, then there is no point debating the meaning of life or how to live, as life itself would not exist.

Second, I ask you to accept that we know "a posteriori" or from experience that the physical world as sensed by our sense organs exists and can be interacted with. Again, I ask you to accept this as an assumed and self-evident truth. While it is certainly true that as Schopenhauer said, the world is not experienced directly but is instead perceived through the understanding as an idea of the world drawn from the sensory organs. It does not matter, as these ideas of reality are shared with a minimum of all others of our kind. This makes them "prima facie" or apparent true representations of reality. While it is conceivable that these mutual perceptions are illusions, we seek the answers to the meaning and purpose of this life and how to live in this world as it is experienced and perceived not any other possible world. Therefore, I ask you to accept the physical universe's existence as a being a fact, "prima facie" and that we can directly perceive and interact with it.

With these agreed truths, we can begin our journey. Let me say right now though, that not all questions are answerable or knowable therefore to find a beginning point; we have to find the first point we can be sure of. We begin with the first mover paradox or what caused the universe to come into being.

Currently, scientific theory points to the big bang as the beginning of the universe, what lead to the creation of the matter that caused the big bang itself is currently unanswerable. It seems likely that this causative chain of beginning is infinite, and with each step which is uncovered, another will likely appear. If we discover the cause of the existence of the matter which caused the big bang the question of what caused that appears and so on forever. This question may seem like a big thing to skip over, and it is. However, the insoluble problem of the first mover eludes all rational explanation and examination. What we are left with is fundamentally guesses and hopes. In the same category also exist such questions as for what purpose was the universe brought into existence? Why did life appear, and if there was nothing to perceive the universe's existence, could it be said to exist? Such first causes are functionally beyond knowing. I'll leave it to you dear reader to proffer whatever hypotheses you think fitting, be they purely physical or involving a deity or pantheon of the divine. As for us and this work, it is enough to say we do not know and move on. Remembering after all that this work seeks to answer the questions of this existence, not of the Supernatural. We aim to answer what our purpose is, and how should we live not to speculate on the unknowable. Falling back onto the two agreed truths that of our existence and the physical world's existence and attesting that beyond that, we know nothing we can truly begin.

The Universe and reality, as we observe it, is governed by complex causal relationships. Understanding these complex relationships are the domain of the sciences. However, in their full scope, they are truly mind-blowing. Consider the chain of events that had to have happened for you to be reading this book today. At its broadest level, the universe had to come into existence, the world had to form around the sun at the exact place it formed, the various extinctions events had to happen, and our species had to develop. Our ancestors had to survive and pass on their DNA over eons, various wars had to be won and lost, knowledge had to be preserved and languages formed. Political and military struggles had to lead to general literacy, and you had to be taught to read. All so as if by chance you could come across this book which owes its existence to many other chains of causation as seemingly unrelated as the myriad events spanning millennium which led you to come across it.

Considering these chains of causation, we are struck by the potentiality of two divergent natures of reality. That of predestination and that of effective chance/fortune. These two possible modes of reality are both possible due to the unknowability of the first cause and the impossibility of accounting for all causative factors throughout time. It is possible that every decision we make is a fait accompli with the outcome decided beforehand. However, it is also possible that the choices we make are constrained by nothing more than the effectively random interaction of millions of events. How do we decide? This problem is where the rules we established at the beginning of our search come in. To decide which metaphysic, we will believe we must apply the rule that any principle must flow logically from a previous principle or from self-evident truth. At this point, we only know three things. One, we don't know the first cause, two we exist and three we exist in a physical world which can be interacted with.

These three truths taken together point us towards the assumption that our universe is governed by effective chance/fortune. The reasons for this are that while we can no more rule out predestination than we can rule out the existence of a deity as the first mover. Logically, there would need to be a universal conscious for there to be predestination. As we only know that the universe can be interacted with as it is physical, and we know that we exist. We are bound by the rule of previous principle/truth. We are prohibited from admitting a principle that relies on an unknown. Therefore, we must accept that while predestination may govern the universe, it is more probable based on our agreed truths that the universe is governed by what amounts to Chance and causation.

By this, we mean that each of us has limited freedom. We can control our actions and interact with the world around us. As a consequence of these actions, we create new chains of causation which interact with and affect the world around us. In the same way, as our actions affect others, we are impacted by, and our freedom is constrained by the effects of other people's choices; the interaction of events outside our control and the effects of past decisions on us. What this means in practice is that while we can influence events, much of life is determined by chance/fortune.

This brings us to the knowledge of three things. One, that we exist, two that the physical world exists and three, that the universe is ruled by the interaction of Chance/Fortune and limited free will. The next step on our journey is to determine our relationship with all other things in existence.

3

Metaphysical Anthropology

Metaphysical anthropology seeks to answer what is man. We are seeking to understand the relationship between ourselves and the rest of reality. If we are part of nature or separate from it. If we are more than or less than other beings. In essence, what is our place in the universe? To determine this, we must first compare ourselves to the other things in the universe, using what we know to be true to determine the answers we seek. So, what do we know?

We know 'a posteriori' (from experience) that we can actively interact with and influence the physical world around us. We can know from observation that there appear to be many different things in this physical world. Some of these things can interact with us, and some of these things cannot. We can also know through observation that many of these things are different from us. In this manner, we can determine that we are somehow distinct from other things.

We also know that there exist things in the world that lack the

13

ability to interact with the physical world. This determination means that we can logically divide the world into two classes of things. Those things that can actively interact with the world, which we shall call beings, and those that cannot, which we will persist in calling things. By actively interact, we mean interact as of their own volition or agency. This quality of agency is what we commonly term as life, with the being possessing it called 'living', while the lack of this quality is termed not life (¬Life), with the thing being called 'non-living'. As such, it is correct to say that all living beings are capable of interaction through their own agency while all non-living things are able to affect the world only through the interaction of an external force.

Through observation, we can also determine that we and all other beings come from the bodies of other beings similar to ourselves, and that after a period of agency, we become things. Which is to say we become incapable of agency upon death. This determination tells us that we go from mere things prior to life, become living beings for a finite period, and then become things once more upon death. This tells us that we are living creatures who live for a time and then will die.

All this may seem obvious, yet it is vital to our understanding of the world and how we answer the big questions. When we add these truths to what we already know, we realise several important things. Firstly, that in the universe in which our existence is experienced, we can deduce from observation that there are multiple sperate things. Some of which are us and some of which are not. Secondly, we can infer from observation that some of those things, which we call beings, can actively interact with things and beings. This dichotomy implies a distinction between beings and things, a difference we call the quality of life. We can also know from experience that we are able to actively interact with other beings and things in the universe. From this, we know we are what we have termed as a being, which is to say we are alive. Thirdly, we can know from observation that beings come from similar beings and are made up of things and become things once more after a finite period (a process called death). From this observation, we can infer the knowledge of our mortality.

In short, these three truths lead us to know that we are an individual being in a universe inhabited by other beings and made up of things. That there is a commonality between ourselves and other beings and that we will, at some point, cease to be a being and become a thing. Knowing these truths allows us to know that we exist as one of many individual beings within a physical universe and are alive for an indeterminate period of time. The question that follows from these truths is that of our relationship between ourselves and the other beings whose existence we can infer from our senses.

The Relationship Between Beings

To determine this relationship, we rely on our faculties of observation and categorise the different beings based on their attributes. By doing this, we discover that the myriad of differences that exist in the other beings are fundamentally ones of degree. Some are bigger, some are smaller. Some are smarter, and some are dumber. Some move in the air, some on land and some in water. Some are faster, and some are slower. Some are more similar to us, and some are less similar. However, in the end, the differences pale beside the difference between the living and the dead, the beings and the things.

Let us examine this a bit more. We naturally assume that we—you, I, the individual at the centre of each of our experience—are the model of normalcy. The yardstick by which to measure all other beings, and why not? We are each one of us, the focus of our own existences. Suppose I have six fingers? Who is to say that five is better or more normal? Bugs are small and alien to me as a human, yet if I were a bug, humans would be huge and just as alien. If I were a tree, would I not perceive as a tree does and (projecting human conceptions of perception on to a plant) would I not find animals to be as unknowable as plants are to us? My point is that we perceive other beings from our own unique perspective. We know this just as we know that, try as we might, this is the only perspective we can see from. To paraphrase Thomas Nagel in his 1974 article for the Philosophical Review, 'We might be able to imagine being a bat, yet we can't know what a bat's experience is like'. Likewise, while we can communicate more easily with other humans compared with plants or bats, we cannot positively know what their experience is like any more than we can 'know' the proverbial bat's experience. This should give us pause for thought.

We know we exist and that other beings exist, yet we cannot know how they perceive the world. The only thing we can say with certainty is that they are alive like us but differ from us by different degrees. These degrees of differentiation may be considerable as between humans and oaks or small as between two types of moth. However, in their essential nature, they are small compared to the difference between things and beings. As we cannot experience life from another being's perspective, it is impossible to judge with any certainty if we are greater or lesser than them. After all, while we can judge that a monkey is indeed better at climbing than us, and that we alone of the other beings can build cities and write literature, we cannot know if their experience is more or less than ours. I posit that all we can say with certainty is that we and other beings are alive and share some commonality with each other.

The Value of Life

With this universal commonality being understood, we are forced to move on to the question of being/life. We have discovered life is the attribute of active interaction with the physical universe. We have also observed that beings are only alive or capable of active interaction for a finite period of time. This transient nature of agency prompts the question: is it better to be or not to be? To answer this question, we need only to observe the universe and consult our own perspective. Through observation and internal consultation, we can all assert that continuance of being is an absolute imperative to us, and from what we can observe, of all other beings. This desire for continuance is another inferred truth: beings who are alive seek (if they seek anything) to continue to exist. This, combined with the other truths, tells us that we exist in a physical universe containing many objects divided into living beings and non-living things. That we are a living being, that like all beings, we will die, and that we desire to continue living.

This universality of the desire (if it may be called a desire) amongst beings to continue living, coupled with the inability to divide beings from each other due to the lack of any measure except yourself, creates an implication that life has, at least from the universal perspective, a uniform value. After all, as I cannot know the perspective of any other being, it stands to reason that just as I judge existence against myself, all other beings must do the same in their own fashion. Prioritising their own existence over other beings just as I do, and judging that which harms them as 'a bad' and that which helps them as 'a good' in the same way as I do. This is not to project cognition on to non-sentient beings, but it is to consider that just as we strive to survive, so do all other living beings. If we accept this universality of the desire for existence, then removing ourselves from our own perspective, we should be able to comprehend the universality or the equality of the value of life.

The concept of equality of life's value at the universal level is not to be confused with implying a proposition that life has no innate value $[A \neq (\neg A)]$. The opposite proposition is intended. Namely, all life has equal value if seen from the universal perspective, which is to be understood as being synonymous with that of a 'Deist God' being able to perceive all life forms simultaneously. The survival of any one species or individual is irrelevant so long as life plural continues while, from the perspective of any individual being, their existence is paramount.

While this does not prove that this value is greater than none (>0) as the premise of this work is that the continuation of life is a universal desire of all beings, there is held to be an implication from this premise that life must have a greater value than not life (). Leaving aside the unanswerable question of the exact value of life, we can for convenience give life a value of 1 and a value of <1. We can also infer that, as each individual being seeks the continuation of existence, they will value their existence above other beings unless it will (as paradoxical as it sounds) result in their own continuation.

This concept of the primacy of individual perspective, or 'per-spectivism' for short, is an important one in this work. It will form the basis for much of what follows from here on in. In review, it is vital that we understand the truths as we know them. Namely, we are separate beings, existing in a physical universe in which there are many objects divided into beings with life and things without. Each of the beings in existence will exist as a being for only a finite period and will become a thing or collection of things once more. Each being seeks the continuation of its existence and can only observe the world from its own perspective. Having thus determined our relationship to the universe and all that is in it, it is time to move onto the big question—the meaning and purpose of life.

4

The Meaning of Life

'The meaning of the world must lie outside of the world. In the world everything happens by chance or accident. As that which is accidental is meaningless. That which makes the world non-accidental or by extension meaningful must therefore lie outside of the world otherwise it would be accidental and therefore meaningless.'

Ludwig Wittgenstein - Tractatus Logico Philosophicus

The meaning of life is often confused with the purpose of life. The difference between the two may seem small at first. However, they are vastly different. The meaning is the 'why'; the purpose is the 'what for'. As such, when we talk of the meaning of life, we are, in essence, asking why we exist or why we are alive. We are not asking what it is that we exist for or what the purpose of life is.

When we ask why we exist or why we are alive, we are only asking part of the question that we should be asking. The real question is not 'why do I or we exist?' but rather, 'why does life exist?'. This question is the genesis of the 'why' questions or the questions of meaning regarding life. It is logical that for us to be able to answer why we exist; we must first answer why life exists. Now, this is a hard question to answer. The greatest thinkers of the ages have tried to answer it and, in many cases, have become confused and ended up talking about the purpose of life as opposed to the meaning of life. This confusion has been the case of most for the theistic religions which have made great stock in answering what we should do but struggled to answer why we should do it (using logical arguments), the 'why'. The reason for this is, as Ludwig Wittgenstein said in his 'Tractatus Logico Philosophicus', 'The meaning of the world must lie outside of the world. In the world everything happens by chance or accident. As that which is accidental is meaningless. That which makes the world non-accidental or by extension meaningful must therefore lie outside of the world otherwise it would be accidental and therefore mean-ingless'. This externality of meaning creates the problem so well comprehended by the Nihilists and Existentialists even if they missed Wittgenstein's conclusion. That of the apparent meaningless of the existence of life. Or more aptly, that the meaning of an event is predicated on the observer's perspective and, as such, has no objective meaning.

The Existentialists took this evident truth as gospel, creating as a by-product the modern sense of purposelessness. However, if we recognise that if there is anything that makes the universe or life ultimately meaningful, it is to be found outside of the physical universe, we begin to understand why we struggle to answer the question of why life or we exist. If the meaning of this universe's existence is only to be found outside of this universe, then the meaning of life's existence is comprehensible only from outside of the universe, and consequently, outside of life.

This conclusion might sound a little bit out there, but hear me out. Let us reduce our question of the meaning of existence down from the ultimate question to one far more benign. Let us consider the existence of a mug. Imagine a mug capable of reflection, asking "why do I exist?". How would one answer this question from the mug's perspective?

Well, let us get specific. When the mug asks, 'why do I exist?' it asks why it exists in this location in space and at this point in time. 'Why do mug's like me exist and what is the meaning of my existence?' If the mug can reflect, we must assume it also has some sense of time stretching from it first being a mug and ending when it ceases to be a mug. It also has a sense of objects not itself in the world such as a table or the seemingly random force which interacts with it. With these truths in hand, it asks itself, 'what is the meaning of my existence or why do I exist?'

Consider also that it will be aware that it may sometimes be hot, or cold, full, or empty, moved, or unmoved. What meaning could it draw from these occurrences? It may be aware that other cups are also prey to these occurrences to either greater or lesser degrees. Again, what meaning can it draw from these happenings? I posit that, like us in life, the mug limited by its perspective would be bound to come up with many of the same ideas we humans have come up with.

It may decide that its existence is meaningless (nihilism), and it does not matter what state it is in as all are neutral. Or it may determine that the meaning of the chance events is determined by it (Existentialism and Stoicism) choosing to regard one state or all states as good or bad, depending on its whim. It may determine that the meaning of existence is to enjoy the pleasant moments (Hedonism and Epicureanism) where it finds them valuing the pleasant states and avoiding the unpleasant ones. It may wonder if the answer to its existence is to be found in the existence of the table it rests on (as we do with the existence of the universe).

Yet as it can only examine the existence of the table from its own perspective, it is locked in a loop. The table exists so that the mug may exist on it at that point in time, and the mug can only exist there as the table exists ad infinitum. As it looks at existence from its own perspective, it could never answer the 'why' of its existence with any certainty. To answer that, it would need to be able to see existence from outside of the existence of things, and in this case, from the perspective of us, its creator.

From our (human) perspective, the why of a mug is simple. The mug exists at that location and point in time because we willed it to exist. The mug was created because we humans desire hot drinks and found that using that ceramic with a handle allowed us to enjoy them. As you enjoy hot drinks in general and desired one at some point in time, the mug came into being, was acquired by you, and was placed in the location where it found itself. The meaning of its existence is that you desired a hot drink. Hence in the completion of this desire, you placed the mug in its present location. This banality explains the why of the cup's existence. If you did not desire hot drinks, you would not have acquired the mug, if you did not desire a drink when you did, the mug would not be where it was, and so on and so forth.

If we return to ourselves, we see that, like the mug, we are trapped in our perspective, or more aptly, in the perspective of life. We look at the physical universe and wonder why it exists. Yet like Schopenhauer in The World as Will and Idea (vol1), we are forced to concede that 'the universe can be said to exist only if it is perceived and it can be perceived only if life exists. But life can only exist if the physical universe has preceded it in time'. This looping nature of the universe from the perspective of life is inescapable in the same way as the table's existence is from the cups. We know we could only exist if the physical universe existed prior to our perceiving it. Yet we can also see that, logically, the physical universe could only be known to exist if it was perceived to exist.

The problem is, we are inside the universe and can therefore not perceive the why of its existence. We are alive and thus cannot perceive the why for life. This conclusion is not to pass judgement as to if there is or is not a why. But merely to state that it is unknowable through observation of the physical universe. It may be possible to determine cosmic truths through communion with the mystical, but that is beyond the scope of this work which is focused on the determination of how to live well in this physical world. Instead of pursuing the unknowable, let us turn our minds to that which can be known with certainty—the 'what for' of life or the purpose of life.

5

The Purpose of Life

"You only live once but you do it right ONCE IS ENOUGH."
Anonymous

The purpose of existence or the 'summum bonum' (greatest good) of life is the subject of our next enquiry. In this examination, we follow the same rules as we have all along. One, that any principle must flow logically from a previous principle or a self-evident truth, and two, that no principle can contradict any other principle. To this end, we must return to the truths that we have discovered and examine them to see if we can discern the purpose from them. Firstly, we know that we exist.

As we exist, any purpose which there is to existence must rely on our existing. There can be no purpose to living if living is not a predicate of that purpose. A way to think of this is to ask, what would the purpose of a light be if nothing could see? It could go on shining, but nothing would come from it. Once something can perceive the light, it can mean something. Through perception, it becomes. In the same way we can view existence, the universe unperceived is irrelevant that it exists or does not in a real way is reliant on something perceiving it. From this logic, we can infer that part of life's meaning to at least things that exist is existence.

Next, we know that in the universe, there are two types of objects; things which can only react to external force, and beings which can interact as of their own volition. Building upon the first principles that meaning follows existence, we can infer that the meaning of life involves interaction to some purpose with other beings and things.

It may not be immediately clear why this must be so. It is thus, as agency or the ability to interact with externals, is part of the fundamental nature of life. It is helpful in understanding this to turn back to that titular sentient mug and ask what is essential in a mug. In other words, what makes a mug = mug, and not a mug = ¬mug. In the case of a mug, its essential nature is being able to hold fluids, be drunk from, and handle. If it lacks a handle, is unable to be drunk from or cannot hold fluids, it ceases to be a mug, and it becomes. This condition is signified by the familiar terms 'broken mug', 'cracked mug', etc. In the case of life, the essential property is being able to independently interact with things external to the being. The absence of this property is considered death or ¬life.

Some of you may blanch at this and point out that this is an inference based upon nothing more than that we are beings, not things. To this, I counter, imagine if we were things, even things with perception, how could we have an independent purpose if we lack the ability to actively influence other things? Without independent action, there can be no purpose, only reaction. A man blown by a storm moves without purpose but simply reacts to the external force. A man walking under no compulsion has purpose, the difference being that one is active and the other is passive.

Putting these two principles together, we can gather that what purpose there is must involve existence and independent action. Next, we consider that, as we are only capable of action for a finite time, after which we become a thing once more, we must conclude that the purpose to our existence must be found in the period of what is called 'life'. This conclusion follows if we consider the need for existence and ability to act from criterion, which is only present in 'life'.

Next, we consider the final thing we know, that each being is an individual who is limited to their own perspective and experience. We can infer from this that the purpose must be common to all beings or living things. This presumption follows as we have deduced that there is no fundamental difference between beings themselves. There exist only relative differences in size, complexity, cognition and form. Putting these together, we see that the meaning of life must be related to life in this physical universe and be common to all beings. What is common to all beings? The desire to continue living!

At first glance, this seems to be a paradox, we know that all beings die, yet we find that the only commonality is the desire to continue living. Yet again, if we observe all beings, we can see other commonalities in their overall behaviour. All beings from the simplest to the most complex undertake actions such as feeding, drinking, and breathing with the aim of continuing to exist. The forms of these actions are as diverse as the forms of the beings themselves. If we continue to observe them, we will undoubtedly notice another commonality. At first, blush does not seem to relate to the continuance of their own existence directly and, in some cases, hastens their demise. This universal behaviour is reproduction.

Reproduction does not make much sense when considered from a purely logical standpoint. In every case, reproduction requires the expenditure of often scarce resources. Resources that would often more logically be expended on the sustainment of the individual being. Why do we do it? As beings capable of logic and reason, we feel compelled to reproduce just as the most primitive microbes do. This paradox is doubled in the case of beings who sacrifice their own lives in the process of reproduction. Why do they do this? We and all other beings do this to continue to exist!

This conclusion may seem paradoxical. After all, how can we exist if we cease to exist? The answer lies in the limitations inherent in mortality. We as beings want to continue to exist/live yet we are doomed to die. As this is unavoidable, we look for the next best thing. What is the next best thing? It is the partial or secondary immortality, offered by passing on our genetic material through reproduction. This statement may seem crude, yet remember we are talking about all beings, not just ourselves. If you were destined to live but for a moment, then cease to exist, is it better if some part of you goes on or none of you? This desire (for lack of a better term) to continue to exist where existence is impossible is a universal absolute. It is manifested in all beings in the desire to reproduce. This compulsion is as true in the most primitive lifeforms as in the more advanced ones such as you and I.

Some readers may take pause at this claim and say, 'But I have never felt the desire to reproduce', or 'I know people who don't want children'. Of course, this may all be true, but it does not invalidate the point. It is an incontestable fact that living things are compelled to reproduce, often without being consciously aware of it. While we cannot know for sure, we can be confident that amoebas do not debate within themselves the pros and cons of reproduction, they just do it. It is also easily verifiable through observation that many animals are suddenly struck by the desire to reproduce through no obvious decision of their own. The world is intrigued by various insects that consume their mates; we are inspired and horrified by the devotion of the parents who sacrifice their own lives for the survival of their young. In us humans, who as of yet are the only species capable of coherently expressing their experience of existence, we can observe that while many of us consciously profess otherwise, most of us will have children. In fact, this desire to reproduce is so absolute in us that even as the rational part of our mind professes to have no desire to reproduce, we still desire sex or channel the desire to continue to exist into the pursuit of power or fame, or even into the creation of art or literature by which we hope to make our mark on the world. But try as we might, death and oblivion still comes to us all.

6

The Purpose of Life Universal

If we step away from ourselves and take a universal view of life, we may see clearer. Looking at all the myriad beings coming into being and ceasing to be at any given moment, we can easily imagine life in all its forms as being almost a single entity. This single entity would, like each individual being, have one primary desire—the desire to continue existing. In essence, this is, as while one living being exists, life exists. If viewed from the universal, it is life as a totality which matters. The individual species and individuals that make up the whole are of little account in the universal schema. It is only the continuation of the universal 'life' that matters, not the continuation of any one individual being or species. As all beings die, new beings are required to continue life, and so new beings must be created in the only way possible, through reproduction. Life, if imagined as a single entity, can be seen to be driven by this desire to continue existing to evolve new forms and to encourage successful reproduction and the spread of life to avoid ending or ceasing to exist. It is this level here that we see the true purpose of all life. That purpose is simply to continue. I repeat it; the purpose of life is to continue.

At this point, many of you may be taken aback. Is it not a cop-out to explain away the purpose of life so glibly? You will be forgiven for thinking such, but you are mistaken. In metaphysics, we talked about the unknowability of the first-mover problem. We recognised that the ultimate reason or the 'why' for the existence of the universe and the appearance of life in it are (if they exist), by their nature, beyond the perception of beings such as ourselves. As these questions were beyond answering, we limited ourselves to the things we did know. Namely, we exist and can interact with other beings and things in this physical universe. This conclusion, by its nature, limits us and this work to the bounds of the physical universe. With this logical limitation, we ignore the unknowable and ask what the purpose of life in this physical universe is. In the case of life universal, it is evident that its driving force is the continuation of existence. This determination is logically consistent with the logical necessities developed in this chapter, namely that the purpose of life must 1. Lie within existence in this physical universe, 2. It must depend on life, and 3. It must be common to all beings. Therefore, we must accept that the purpose of life is to live and the greatest good (summum bonum) of existence/life is for existence/life to continue.

7

The Purpose from the Perspective of the Species

If we descend from the universal perspective to the perspective of a single species, is the view not the same? If we imagine each species as being as a single individual, would that being not desire only to continue existing? Would that individual species not mirror the universal by developing new adaptions to the environment, seeking to spread its range and enhance its survival? At the species level, again, it is only the survival of the species that matters. The individual which constitutes the whole is essential only as far as it contributes to the survival of the whole. The species abstracted as an individual seeks to survive and is yet made up of mortal beings. So, to continue to exist, the beings within it must reproduce for the species to survive. This conclusion implies that the purpose of the species is the same as that of life universal if only more specific. While life universal seeks only for life to continue, the species abstracted seeks only for the species to survive. The only way that a species can survive is via successful reproduction. What do we mean by successful reproduction? We mean the production of healthy offspring who survive to reproduce themselves.

How each species and the individual beings that make up those species achieve this grand purpose are as different as the individual species are from each other. With reproduction, some beings such as aphids or quaking aspen trees effectively clone themselves. Others such as many fish lay eggs and have thousands of young surviving through numbers alone. Still others, such as most mammals, have small numbers of young and care for them for extended periods of time. Each species also approaches the survival of their members to allow for successful reproduction in diverse ways. Some species opt to survive alone, others form complex social groups with kin, while others have developed a symbiotic relationship with other species. However, as different the means may be, the purpose is the same, to continue life through successful reproduction.

8

The Purpose from the Individual Perspective

As we return to our own level, we can view our particular purpose. In the same way as life universal and the 'abstracted' species seek only the continuation of our own existence. However, just like the higher orders of life, we are incapable of meeting that aim except by reproduction or the successful transmission of our genes through other means. This requirement implies that the purpose of all beings is to seek to survive and ensure the survival of their genes. In this way, the Individual Purpose of the individual being is interrelated to, yet more specific than that of the species to which it belongs. The individual being is the lowest level of life. Its survival and its genome's survival are vitally important to itself but less important to the species as a totality.

In nature, not all beings can reproduce, and in some cases, it is even better for the species as a whole that they do not. Just as individual beings perish without the notice of their species, so too do species disappear without notice from the innumerable multitude of life. This ongoing holocaust is to be understood through the prism of the universal value of life at the universal level. Each being values itself absolutely, this is as true of the ant as of the man. From a universal perspective, both are the same; they are life. That a man may crush an ant is nothing to life universal and little to the man. Yet to the ant, it is the end of everything. Just so a bacterium may overwhelm a man, being seen as a great evil by him, yet to the bacterium, it is merely a necessity of life, and again to life universal, it is only life continuing.

You may wonder now that if the purpose and highest good of life is to reproduce, am I suggesting that we humans have no other reason for living? Are we expected to make babies and die? Well, the answer is both yes and no. Yes, for many or most of us humans, the Individual Purpose will compel us to have children (and what a joy that is). Yet, it will not be possible for others through physical inability or only due to the circumstances in which they find themselves. Nevertheless, that is just a small part of the story. So far, we have talked in abstract terms about beings, life, and the purpose. From now on, we will speak about us in the specific.

9

The Purpose from the Human Perspective

We humans are unique. We are us; we are not like other species. That is not to say that we are above or below other beings, but we are distinct. How we achieve our Individual Purpose is unique to us as a species. If we were ants, we would talk of the Individual Purpose of the ant. Yet as we are humans, we will focus on ourselves.

We, like all other species and beings, seek the continuation of ourselves. The continuation of existence can be achieved primarily by reproduction, or secondarily, through ensuring the survival of genetic relations. Ensuring the survival of our children or our kin is our purpose. It is so simple and straightforward that, for millennium, it has gone unremarked. Every human is guided unconsciously by this purpose, but when the great thinkers of the world contemplated life's meaning, it seems to have escaped their notice. For eons, the philosophers and prophets degraded the instinct to protect family to an inferior station. Promoting unattachment to this world and the physical, in exchange for a supposed reward in some other existence. This impulse was as true for the Stoics and Epicureans as for the Buddhists, Christians, or Muslims today. Each path to purpose, happiness, enlightenment, or salvation was and is supposed to lie in the abandonment (or at least relegation in importance) of the family and the physical world. However, this needs not be the way, the purpose of life may be simple; however, its achievement is far from easy.

Our purpose is not as it first seems merely to reproduce. It is to ensure the survival of our genetic line, which forms the unique offshoot of our species. This purpose can only be achieved by ensuring the survival of any children we have and or by ensuring the survival of our close kin, namely our siblings. It is not enough to produce children; we must ensure their survival and the survival of our siblings and their children. How we ensure the survival of this kin is where the complexity comes in.

Each action we take can influence their long-term survival. How we treat other people or beings, how we act at work and at home, if we choose to be part of a community or not. What kind of society we seek to build, what kind of government we allow to govern us, the moral maximins we live by and transmit to our children. Every one of these choices impacts on the long-term survival of our families. In short, if we accept that our purpose as humans is to promote the survival of the human race as represented by our families, then we are obligated to seek the best way of living to achieve that aim.

As beings possessing rationality and intellect, we must utilise those advantages to determine the optimum way to live to achieve our Individual Purpose. It is this search for the optimum that is the proper subject of this book. Before we move on to this, it is necessary to review what we know once more to find where we are. In our examination of existence, we determined that we existed and that we existed in a physical universe. That events in this universe were governed by predictable cause and effect and causative events that we term chance/fortune, which are beyond our prediction. We observed that the objects in this physical universe are divided between the living beings and the non-living things. Finally, we observed that all beings were animated by the same desire to continue existing. This conclusion was seen to be true, be they viewed as a single whole from the universal level, as a grouping of similar beings as a species, or as a single individual being/organism. We deduced that, in all cases, beings being transient (mortal) could only continue to exist through reproduction. From these revelations, we inferred that the highest good and purpose of all beings was to ensure the survival of their species and life itself through ensuring the successful survival of their genetic code, which is the essence of their selves in this physical universe—an aim we coined as their Individual Purpose for short. As we shared a commonality with all other beings, it follows that our purpose as rational beings is to determine how we can best achieve our Individual Purpose based on our own unique advantages and situations. It is how we can accomplish this Individual Purpose which we will now examine.

II

The Path

10

The Self

"Every individual... neither intends to promote the public interest, nor knows how much he is promoting it... he intends only his own security; and by directing that industry in such a manner as its produce may be of the greatest value, he intends only his own gain, and he is in this, as in many other cases, led by an invisible hand to promote an end which was not part of his intention."

Adam Smith - The Wealth of Nations

The individual is central to this work. This work does not espouse a collectivist doctrine that places the group above the individual. It is an individualist philosophy that relies on in-formed self-interest to guide the individual to the achievement of their Individual Purpose, being their family's survival. Let us begin with what we know about the individual being so far. We can infer from the principle of 'perspectivism' that the individual being has an equality of inherent value.

We can deduce that if each being's inherent value is the same from the universal perspective due to its purpose being only the continuation of life in all its forms, then the value each species and being must assign to other beings must also be predicated on the achievement of their purpose. Just as species, if they were able to think, would prioritise their continued existence over others, consequently placing greater value on their existence than others, so too must individual beings.

The Value of the Individual

All beings find themselves at the crux of their own existence. From their perspective, their existence is all, and as such, they value themselves higher than all other beings. This is both natural and correct. To achieve our Individual Purpose, we must generally continue to exist. By placing our own survival first, we allow ourselves to pursue our purpose with clarity. However, we must sound caution here to prevent misunderstanding.

Just as you place yourself first, so to do all others. To you, you are the most valuable being, and to them, they are the most valuable being. This valuation is only a matter of perspective and does not alter the inherent equality of your and their inherent value. It should be a position of faith that each individual has, at their birth, equal latent potential. Every one of us is capable of anything. While genetics play a role in our traits and give us advantages in some areas and weaknesses in others, we must not let them define us. The race is not always to the swift or the fight to the strong.

In a universe, as conceived here governed by choice and chance, we cannot judge with any reliability what potential a person may possess. Who would have picked from the infancies of the great men and women of the ages that they would achieve greatness? Churchill and Hitler were famously considered by their teachers and parents to be unpromising, yet achieved distinction or notoriety in their own ways. Fabius Maximus, who was counted as one of Rome's greatest heroes, was in his youth derided for his meekness and supposed stupidity. So common is this defiance of expectations that luminaries such as Isaac D'Israeli and Rousseau commented on it. With Rousseau going so far as to assert that 'this seeming and deceitful dullness in youth in many cases is the sign of a profound genius'. Therefore, we should take to heart that we are not superior to others except in our own estimations and treat all beings with respect.

How to Achieve Our Purpose

The individual exists in the world as both a single independent entity and as part of a greater whole. As an independent entity, we seek our own interests and welfare, yet as we are also part of a greater whole, we cannot act without affecting others. The difficulty in achieving the deceptively simple purpose of life lies in this. If we accept that our purpose in life is synonymous with that of the Individual Purpose, then we are impelled to seek the best way to achieve it.

As a starting point, we should consider our actions and seek to harmonise them with the achievement of the Individual Purpose. In essence, we should seek to expend our energies on those activities that will promote our survival and welfare. Conversely, we should resist the temptation to act in ways that we judge as being harmful to our welfare and long-term survival. In practice, this means that we must seek to act in such a way as will promote our achievement of the Individual Purpose while factoring in the often-unconscious way in which all other beings are doing the same and the cumulative effect these concurrent actions have on the achievement of your Individual Purpose.

For us as humans, this means taking the time to reflect on the actions we are taking to see how they affect the world around us, the other beings we share the world with, and how they affect us. This is due to the ability of our actions to lead to unbudgeted externalities. For instance, if we act in a way that while initially beneficial to ourselves leads to long-term negative consequences that harm our long-term interests, this is harmful. An example of this is the temptation to overfish an area or to take undersized fish. While initially, we benefit from the surplus, the long-term impact is a reduction in the fish stocks and diminishing returns. By acting unreflectively, we harm our long-term interests, and through our inattention or caprice, harm other beings which are then incentivised to retaliate against us.

As individuals, we can exert the most significant influence over the achievement or non-achievement of our Individual Purpose. However, we cannot achieve it alone. The accomplishment of our Individual Purpose is, like all things in life, only partially in our hands. Our choices influence but cannot decide the issue. In essence, this is due to the nature of existence being partly dependent on our choices and partially dependant on fortune's influence. In the case of the Individual Purpose, it is further complicated as it can only be achieved through successful reproduction, which requires two unrelated individuals.

The question implied by this necessity is as two (generally) unrelated individuals are necessary for the achievement of the Individual Purpose. How are we to act to promote this outcome? Now, of course, some animals have the equivalent of casual sex and leave their offspring at the mercy of fate. However, many others and, in particular, the more complex animals, take a far more active role in the selection of a mate and the rearing of their young. In the Hobbesian war of survival that Darwinian evolution supposes, it beggars belief that these complex behaviours happen by chance and are not productive to those beings' achievement of their Individual Purposes and, consequently, the achievement of the purpose of life universal.

11

The Family

"For better and for worse, family relationships play a central role in shaping an individual's wellbeing across their life course."

Merz, Consedine, Schulze, & Schuengel, 2009

If we examine human society around us in all its diversity, we can glean that one institution is so common as to be universal. From the humans living in the most primitive jungle bands in the wilds of New Guinea to those dwelling in the most modern societies in New York or Hong Kong, the family is a constant. Its scope and the definition of membership may vary, yet at its heart, the family consists of genetically related kin. If we look back through our history, we see that the family remains central to human life be at the dawn of time when humans lived in small bands of hunters and gatherers or in the present day when we live in metropolises. Why does this institution exist everywhere humans do? It exists as it is an effective means of achieving successful reproduction.

What do we mean by family? The definition of a family as it exists in English has several more or less expansive meanings ranging from the narrow interpretation of you and your children to the whole of the human race. For example, the Oxford Dictionary defines family as being:

1. 'A group consisting of two parents and their children living together as a single unit' and

2. As 'a group of people related by blood or marriage'.

Cambridge Dictionary provides a definition that vaguely states that a family is a 'group of people related to each other'. While the Merriam-Webster Dictionary offers an even broader definition ranging from the 'two parents and their children to a group of people deriving from a common stock or ancestor'. These definitions are too vague for our purpose. For clarity of understanding, we will henceforth define family as those individuals who share a close genetic relationship with yourself which we shall define as sharing DNA in the range of 25% of your own.

Families in all societies are governed by implicit rules of behaviour that serve perhaps unknowingly to promote the survival of the family members. Where families function well, they promote the sharing of resources and information to all members' benefit. To prove this point, we only need to look at our own societies.

We exist in an age where data is ubiquitous as such; it is easy to determine the impact that the family has on a child's life chances. Even in highly individualistic Anglo-Saxon nations, academic research indicates that the lack of close family during childhood showed strong correlations with poor life outcomes. These outcomes range from long-term income disadvantage, lower general intelligence levels to poorer physical and mental health. Furthermore, these adverse effects seemed, in many cases, to be inherited by subsequent generations. These extraordinary adverse effects are quite striking. If even in the modern age in countries with high standards of living and advanced societal support systems, these outcomes were still pronounced, then it must have been even more so in the past. This was easily confirmed, every author from the past who dealt with the plight of the forgotten talk about the orphan and the widow's sorrow. Victor Hugo, a French author and historian, mentions the figure of '50% of abandoned children perishing' in nineteenth-century Paris. The bible mentions the suffering of those without families often, and let's not forget the suffering of the Wolfskinder or parentless children from Germany after the second world war.

By reviewing the evident negative effect of lack of family on children's survival and life outcomes, it is apparent that the family makes a substantial contribution to human offspring's survival. Furthermore, these laudatory effects are not limited to childhood but continue throughout life with the positive impact of families being correlated with greater stress resistance in adults and increased longevity in seniors. As our purpose is to ensure the survival of ourselves, our children, and our kin, and as the institution of family supports this aim, it is clear that it must form part of our Individual Purpose.

We should understand that family differs from kin. Family is more than just a group of those who are genetically related to some extent. It is a formalised group which has rules for admission and set obligations for those within it. The family in this work consists of three distinct groupings. Each of the three groupings, while being distinct, have overlapping responsibilities.

The first element of the family is the 'birth family'. The birth family is the nuclear family into which you are born. The birth family is limited to those who share around 25% of your genetic code, extending up to your grandparents and across to include your uncles and aunts.

Birth Family

The first element of the family is the 'Birth Family'. The birth family is the nuclear family into which you are born. The birth family is limited to those who share around 25% of your genetic Code extending up to your grandparents and across to include your uncles and Aunts.

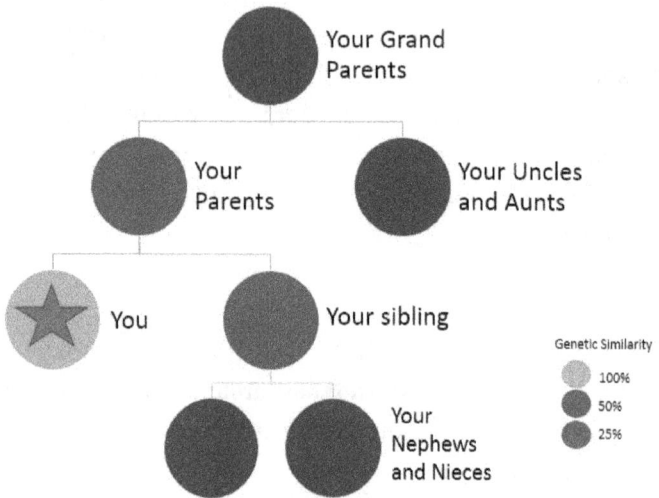

Figure 1: Birth Family

Reproductive Family

The second and more critical grouping is the 'Reproductive Family' or your nuclear family. This second family is the family which you form when you and a partner produce offspring. This family extends downwards to your grandchildren who share an approximate genetic closeness of 25% with yourself.

Genetic Similarity

100%

50%

25%

Your Spouse

You

Your Childs Spouse

Your Children

Your Grand Children

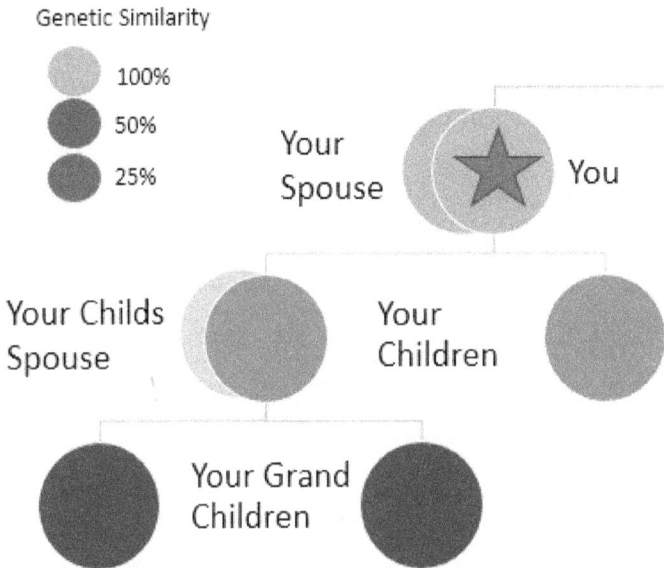

Figure 2: Reproductive Family

Combined, the conception of the two genetic families in the Code is similar to the more ancient concept of consanguinity. Yet it is not the same, as the degrees of consanguinity do not precisely align with genetic closeness. For example, while you share approximately 50% of your DNA with both your parents and siblings, their degrees of consanguinity are one for your parents and two for your siblings. The diagram below better illustrates this distinction and visually defines the family in the conception of the Code.

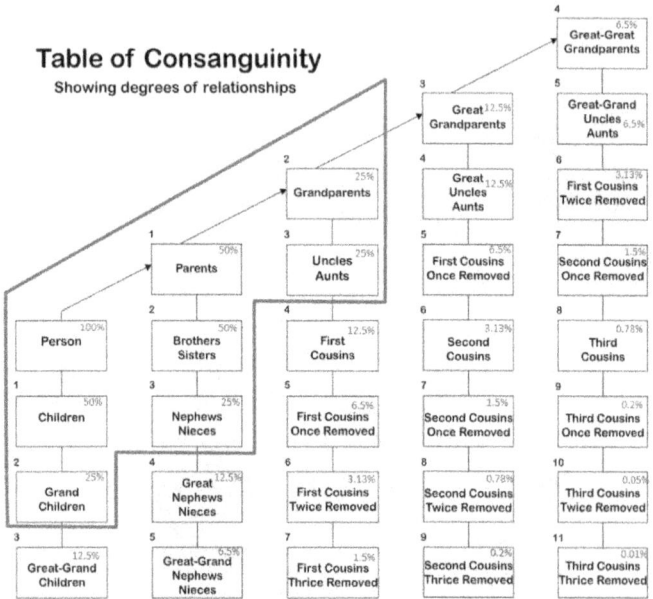

Figure 3: Consanguinity vs Family

However, this is only one part of the family. As we reproduce sexually, we almost inevitably expand our families to include our reproductive partners. This expansion makes sense as, in essence, by producing children with another individual, you create a new family as those children share 50% of their genetic material with your family and 50% with their other parent. It follows that as you and your partner create this new family, you both bring with you your existing familial connections. As children follow, both you and your partner's relations have a vested interest in the survival of your children. But what of your obligations to your partner and their kin? While they are not related to you, they share a duty to your partner and your children. This problem is an ancient one and is resolved in our society through the institution of families-in-law.

Family In-Law

In this work, this problem is managed through the third element, which is also called the 'Family In-law'. This third element of the family consists of the addition of your partner's birth family to yours. In essence, upon marriage, the two partners reciprocally assume each other's duties to their respective families. I.e. her mother and father become your father and mother and vice versa. This union of families is only through the two of you and your children. It does not extend to either of your birth families. In other words, while you and your partner have duties to each other's families and both families have duties to the two of you, the two families' members do not incur any duties to each other.

This can be seen in the diagram below whereby, through marriage, your family expands to include your spouse's kin but your and their families only expand to include yourselves and any offspring you have. Each birth family includes the new nuclear family but not each other.

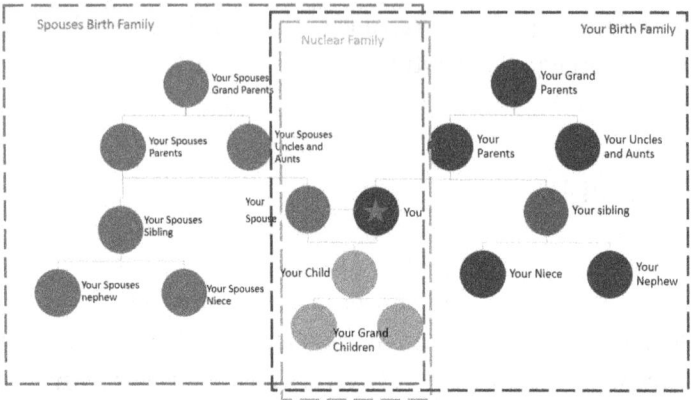

Figure 4: Family Circles

12

Duties to Family

The family should provide that critical support to each other, ensuring that they collectively can survive and that they and their offspring can achieve their Individual Purposes by re-producing successfully. So, what are our obligations to our families? If we consider that our purpose is to ensure our genes' survival and that our family members carry our genes, then it logically follows that we must protect our families from harm. This is the first duty, 'protect your family'. This duty, like the Individual Purpose, sounds deceptively simple yet is complicated in practice. It is important to note that duties are minimum standards of behaviour. They are not catch all's but are intended to set a limit by which, if an individual refrains from acting, they jeopardise their Individual Purpose's achievement.

Physical protection is, of course, mandatory, but protection does not stop there. Protecting is an active duty, not a passive one. It is not sufficient to await danger and respond when it appears. You are required to anticipate threats to your family's long-term survival and act to prevent them from becoming a reality. This duty includes ensuring their physical safety by providing sufficient food, shelter, and physical security. However, it is not limited to merely physical enemies and dangers but extends to anything that can bring them harm if done or not done. Some examples could include financial risks such as gambling on risky investments or not having life insurance to provide for them if you were to die. Allowing yourself to abuse drugs or alcohol or spend money on frivolous things or cheat on your partner. It includes seemingly unrelated decisions such as investing in an education or settling for a dead-end job. If you take a less comfortable job which pays well or choose a more comfortable job which does not. If you choose to work out and eat well or if you don't. If you expend your efforts to improve the world around you or you don't, and even how you treat others. All these actions and much more influence the world around you and impacts upon your family's long-term welfare and survival. Our duty is to seek the best decisions and actions to achieve our Individual Purpose and protect our families.

To provide greater clarity, we can boil the duty to protect our family down into the following elements.

To Protect Them Physically

This element places an explicit obligation on yourself and all other family members to actively take all reasonable steps to prevent physical attacks on your family members. This duty is an active obligation, meaning that it is not enough to simply respond after the fact. If that were the case, there would be a duty to avenge, not protect. Instead, the active duty to protect means you are enjoined to use your wisdom and foresight to ensure their safety. This duty is broad in scope as the protection from physical attack can be approached in many different ways depending on the situation you find yourself in.

As a minimum, it means to take personal responsibility for your family's safety by maintaining enough physical strength and resources to defend yourself and your family from physical attack. Depending on the situation, however, this obligation could be supported by means such as supporting the local police in maintaining civil order. Serving in the Defence Forces of your nation to deter foreign aggression, building relationships for mutual defence within your communities. Campaigning for legal or constitutional reforms to increase public security, installing physical alarms and barriers to impede attacks and hiring private security. In more extreme situations, it could involve pre-emptive strikes on those who threaten your family or virtually any multitude of other actions which have as their ultimate aim the protection of your family from physical attack.

Provide Necessities of Life

This element of the duty to protect your family from harm is, again, as with all duties, an active duty. In this case, it lays out the obligation for you to take all reasonable actions to ensure that no member of your family is harmed through the lack of the necessities of life. By the necessities of life, we refer primarily to food, water, and shelter, though they can be extended to any other actual necessity warranted by the situation. This duty is not to be mistaken as an exhortation to some kind of familial socialism. Instead, it is a limited obligation to take on the responsibility to feed and shelter your kin if they are unable to do so themselves. This does not mean that you must ensure that they have the same standard of life as you do, only that you cannot sit by while they starve, freeze, or otherwise suffer harm which you could prevent.

Provide Emotional Support

The third element of the duty to protect is emotional, not physical. This duty is easily overlooked yet is often vital for protecting our families from harm. This duty boils down to simply being there for your family members. Making yourself available to talk, listen, and care. Checking in on them (regardless of if they are a chore) and making sure they know that someone is there for them. Loneliness is a killer, and while it is less visible than violence or want, it can be a threat to our families just as easily.

Our duty here is to be there for our family members. To make the effort to reach out to them and support them to be their unconditional supports and honest friends. Family can often be challenging, and you do not get to choose who is in it. Members of your family are certainly going to make choices that you disagree with, act immorally, or even wrong you. However, this does not excuse your duty towards them.

While you must protect yourself and those you have a duty to within these limits, you must still attempt to be there for those in your family. If possible, try and guide them to better choices, but if not, at least ensure that they know that you are still there for them.

We must provide the first and most constant support to our families because they and we should be each other's most reliable supports in the world. Of course, the family, while vital, only tells part of the story of the achievement of our Individual Purposes. There are other people in the world other than our kin, and our families-in-law have to come from somewhere. This other is the community.

13

The Community

"No man is an island, entire of itself; every man is a piece of the continent, a part of the main. If a clod be washed away by the sea, Europe is the less, as well as if a promontory were, as well as if a manor of thy friend's or of thine own were: any man's death diminishes me, because I am involved in mankind, and therefore never send to know for whom the bells tolls; it tolls for thee."

John Donne, No Man is an Island, A Selection from the Prose.

The community forms the second distinct layer of reciprocal obligation. Its function in the individual's achievement of the Individual Purpose is analogous to that of the extended family (birth family and spouse's birth family), however, it differs in that the ties are more tenuous, and the obligations are based on the principle of reciprocity as opposed to the direct achievement of the Individual Purpose as found in the family. While it may have overlapping membership with the extended family, the community is fundamentally separate and distinct. Consisting of the combination of individual families for mutual support in achieving their own Individual Purposes.

The community exists only to support the survival of the constituent families. As such, membership of the community is predicated on the continuing support of each citizen of the said community for the survival of the other families/citizens in the community. So-called communities that lack this nature are not communities at all but rather collections of individual families or, at most, collections of disparate communities. As such, the term 'community' connotes only groups of families/citizens who recognise mutual standards of behaviour and the reciprocal obligations to each other. This is the meaning of community from here on in.

14

Membership of the Community

A community can be small or large; it can involve people separated by space or those who are not. The community exists due to the duties to each other, which the members acknowledge, and is continued by the fulfilment of those same duties. To be part of a community, as the definition of community connotes, requires the individual to consent to act in such a way as to enhance the survival of the other citizens of the community and their families. As well as refrain from acting in any way which harms the survival of the other citizens. Therefore, membership of the community is predicated on three conditions: exclusivity, affirmation, and mutual recognition of members.

Exclusivity

The obligation to act to enhance the survival of the other citizens and refrain from acting in any way that harms the survival of the other citizens is ultimately exclusive in nature. This exclusivity may seem counter-intuitive in an age whose bywords are transnationalism and cosmopolitanism. However, citizenship, like membership in a family, carries with it non-negotiable duties. Duties are absolutes, contingent only upon higher duties. To allow for a multiplicity of absolute obligations to divergent and competing groups would be highly illogical. It would require a citizen to attempt to prioritise between two groups that had equal claims to their loyalty. If the individual was required to harm one to protect the other, which would they choose?

Of course, in most cases, being loyal to a community will not involve harm to another community. However, one cannot merely consider the demands of peace but also the needs of crises. To be a citizen of multiple communities is to be, in a real way, a citizen of none. Wherever loyalty is divided, it is in doubt because if you are forced to choose between the two equals, the question must be by its nature doubtful. As such, citizenship of a community must be exclusive and singular if it is to be relied upon. Citizenship must supersede any other claim for loyalty except for that to the family. In addition to being exclusive, citizenship must also be predicated on the acceptance of the obligations of citizenship.

Affirmation

The acceptance of citizenship obligations must be an active affirmation, not a passive submission. With the claim to exclusivity of citizenship, it also follows that the individual members of a community must actively and freely choose to belong to and actively affirm their acceptance of their duties to the community. As such, no individual can naturally be a citizen by the mere chance of birth in a community. They must become one by affirming it in their majority, choosing to reject any other claims on their loyalty at the same time.

This concept can be conceptualised as follows; a child born in such a society would have the right to affirm their citizenship by virtue of birth or descent but would not be a citizen by birth or descent. Upon reaching an age whereby they are judged to have reached adulthood, they would choose to affirm or not affirm their right to citizenship. If they chose to affirm after renouncing any other citizenships and carrying out whatever service to the community was required, they would be admitted to full citizenship. Suppose they chose not to affirm their citizenship. In that case, they could either remain as a resident or take up without prejudice the rights of citizenship of any other community which they may be entitled.

However, affirmation is not single-sided, it must be mutual. It is naturally contingent on the acceptance of the existing citizens. The existing citizens retain the right to both reject the applicant and expel those who fail in their duties to the group. In our example, the young person had the right to affirm their citizenship and be recognised as a citizen by virtue of birth or descent. In a strangers' case, the principle of qualification would apply.

Recognition

This acceptance of the existing citizens or, as it will henceforth be called, recognition, is the third of the prerequisites of membership of a community. After all, as the community exists only to promote the constituent families' survival, it is natural that the existing members hold a veto over the inclusion of new citizens and the right to expel miscreants. The requirement of recognition of citizenship provides a failsafe for the community in that it allows for the enforcement of the community's minimum standards in a way in which, without the principle, would not be possible. As such, to become a community member, an individual must actively offer their loyalty to the community without caveat and be recognised by the existing citizens. It follows that the membership of any group that demands loyalty above the community other than the family is unacceptable in our conception of community.

Another example might provide some clarity here. For example, if a stranger wanted to become a citizen of this society, they would need to fulfil the same service required of the young and be allowed by the citizens to join them. Similarly, if an existing citizen betrayed the community by acting in a grievously harmful manner or through the continued membership of a group that required of its members higher loyalty than that to the community, they could be excluded from the community.

15

Nature of the Community

Having determined the requirement for membership of the community, it is now necessary to discuss the nature of the relationship between the citizens inside the community. As in the predicates for membership of the community, the relationship between members of the community must be structured in such a way as to promote the survival of the constituent families. To fulfil this purpose, there are specific characteristics that must be present within the community. Firstly, there must be nominal equality between the citizens.

This is not to imply equality of material wealth, ability, or any other advantages or disadvantages that fortune supplies. It is to indicate only equality of personal value. To this end, there can be no distinction between individuals in a community by class, religion, birth or ancestry. Membership of a community must be based on equality of the person with distinctions drawn only by actions and character. We will discuss distinctions more in book four, but we must understand that to divide citizens in any other way would be to create effectively separate communities out of the previous single community.

Similarly, no citizen can be affiliated with any group that demands loyalty to the group above that of the wider community or which would restrict them from carrying out their duties to the community. This prohibition includes religious groups that demand pacifism (which is a negation of the duty to protect), obedience to the religious heads on temporal matters or any other group that seeks to separate its adherents from the community substantively. In all of these circumstances, the citizen, through their membership of these groups, would be seen to have renounced their citizenship as they could no longer be relied upon to carry out their duties.

16

Duties to the Community

The duties owed to the community by its members are similar in nature to that owed by each person to their family, though necessary lesser in scope. What must be held in mind is that the family has priority over the community, not the other way around. If there is a conflict between the two, the family should win out. This will be spoken about in greater depth later in book three, where we discuss prioritisation. The duties owed to the community are one, that of protection, two, that of assistance, and three, emotional support. These duties are reciprocal and are a requirement for the existence of a community.

To Protect Them Physically

The duty of protection is the first duty owed to the community. This duty is based on the community's primary purpose in promoting the survival of the community members. The duty of protection in the context of the community is one where each member of the community has an obligation to, within the limits of their ability, protect the other members of the community from harm. This obligation is secondary to the duty to protect your family from harm. As such, there is a certain amount of judgement required in the fulfilment of this duty so that you do not unduly risk your family's wellbeing while protecting those in your community. The duty to protect is an active duty being that it is both a duty to act and refrain from acting. Just as I am duty-bound to save or protect someone from my community where I can, I am also duty-bound to avoid acting in such a way as would be likely to cause harm to come to a member of my community unless necessary to the achievement of the purpose.

The essence of this duty relies on the reciprocal relationship, which is inherent in the community. You are obliged to act to protect your community members as they are compelled to act to protect you. It rests not on altruism but on informed self-interest. If you will, a calculation that the risk to yourself and your family of placing yourself at risk to protect the community is less than the risk you and your family would face if they were attacked and nobody helped them. This calculation is at the core of what motivates communal action. We take part if we recognise that we stand to gain more than we lose by taking part. This gain is the same reason we join communities in the first place. We seek our benefit even if we couch it in more noble terms.

For this reason, if we see a stranger being attacked and do not assist them, we accept that when we are attacked, no one should help us. Just as if we saw a person drowning in the ocean and choose not to help them, we are essentially proclaiming that if we were to drown nobody should help us. The actions we take or do not take are the gospels of our Code. Nobody can force anyone else to assume a duty, but everyone can inspire others by their example and create a better world through small, consistent actions.

To Provide Necessities of Life

Similar to the duty to your family, the duty to your community also extends past the simple prevention of physical attacks to ensure that members of your community have the minimum needs of life met regarding food, clothing, and shelter. This duty refers to the minimum standard required to preserve life, not necessarily one that provides for their comfort or pleasure. This impulse is not to be seen to be based on mere sympathy or compassion; instead, it should be seen to be based on self-interest alone.

If you were to have the means to do so yet chose not to provide someone in desperate need with the necessities of life, would they not be likely or even justified in taking those necessities by force? Consider what we have said so far about the duties to family and the innate survival instinct. If you have what someone needs to survive and will not share it, then they will take it if they can. However, it is not just from fear of force by which you should be compelled to provide the necessities of life to those in your community, it should be as with the duty to protect, be drawn from the truth that the person in need could be you.

Keep in mind when you see a person in need, (to paraphrase and secularise) John Bradford's famous saying, 'There but by the caprice of fortune go you'. If you walk by and do not help when you could have, you set the standard for yourself and those you love. By not helping, you say to the world, 'Just as I have not helped a fellow citizen in need so to do not help me when I am in need'.

This duty is not to be understood as an invocation to beggar yourself through charity, or as Peter Singer suggests in A Life You Can Save, 'an obligation without limits on location and relationship'. But, rather a specific duty to take what actions you can without harming your family's welfare or long-term survival chances to ensure that the members of your community do not lack the necessities of life. It is not an obligation on the individual to alleviate the want of everyone in your community. You should see it as the light of a child appearing at your door in a storm. You shelter them for the night and help them find their way home. Or a starving man in the street whom you feed. You help those whom you can, where you can, in the way which you can.

To Provide Emotional Support

As with family, emotional support is vital in protecting the people in your community. Again, this duty does not mean that you are responsible for taking on everyone's problems or sticking your nose into other people's business. However, it does mean that you should, in the confines of your personal bubble, be available to those around you. This can take the form of showing care and concern for your workmates, your neighbours, and those who chance places in your path such as on the train or next to you on a plane.

We all need the support of those around us. We all want to be accepted, included, and valued. By taking the time to care for those around you (especially the difficult people), we can actively contribute to our own good and our communities. Building relationships that assist us in the achievement of our purpose and helping to create a better place to live, work, or study.

This mundane part of your duty may seem unimportant compared to the heroic acts of physical defence or the philanthropic act of providing the necessities of life to one who may perish otherwise. However, it is just as important. This element of your duty achieves its effect not through one or two great acts but from a multitude of little actions.

Taking the time to listen to a workmate's problem or compliment them on a job well done is a small thing. Yet, each one is like a single drop of water in a desert. Each drop alone has but little impact. However, over time, if they continue, those small drops add up. A garden grows where there was only barren dirt, and rain falls where there was none before. By providing emotional support to those around you, you can have a considerable influence.

At first, you may see no effect, but persist and those around you will imitate you and show more care to those around them. The desert of our suburbs and workplaces will flower into real communities.

As you may perceive, there is the potential for there to be conflicts between our duties to our families and our community or between duties to individual members of each. How are we to prioritise between them? How can we reliably determine the individual that will most likely assist us in achieving our purpose at any given time? To do this, we must assign each individual a position in a hierarchical system. By assigning a clear hierarchical position to each duty and individual, it allows for effective and clear prioritisation and forms the basis for the moral calculations in the ethics.

III

The System

17

Prioritisation

"Life is all about priorities. Year after year, day after day, and even minute after minute you have to embrace what is more important and essential for you and not look back. When others don't understand or admonish you for your choices don't give it any energy because they are telling you that their wants are more significant than yours."

Carl Henegan, Darkness Left Undone

Prioritisation is, in essence, the problem of economics or the scarcity of resources at the level of human actions. Like with governmental leaders or a person living on a fixed income in life, we have to decide between competing desires and interests limited by the paucity of resources and time. In the case of moral action, we are limited by our singularity and limited abilities and thus forced to choose between carrying out our duties to one person or group or another. As we must choose, we require a systematic approach to inform our choices.

Hierarchy of Duty

The hierarchy of duty provides a clear and consistent frame-work for decision-making when there are competing duties to two or more people or groups. Providing a logical hierarchy of duty allows adherents to easily prioritise between duties to individuals and duties themselves at all times. The fundamental principle is that the higher up the hierarchy a duty or individual sits, the greater their precedence is. This order of precedence allows for consistency to be maintained, as whenever there are conflicting demands, the relative precedence of the demands can be weighed, and the conflict resolved. Under this system, an individual remains bound to the canon of the duties and to all the individuals who a duty is owed at all times. However, as precedence is clear, if they are physically unable to meet two or more of their responsibilities, they must only meet the superior duty's obligations. This principle is quite self-apparent, yet to be workable while being logically consistent, it requires a method of characterising each individual.

The mechanism that meets this requirement is Relational Proximity (RP). This principle holds that the precedence of a duty or an individual's precedence is directly related to the Individual Purpose, namely the long-term survival of your family. The more vital the object is to the Individual Purpose's achievement, the higher its Relational Proximity is. In calculating an individual's position in this framework, it should be no surprise that those within the family come first, followed by those who are members of your community and, finally, those who have no formal relation to you and your family. We begin with the individual 'subject'.

Relational Proximity Level 1: Family - Primary Branch

The individual 'subject', or simply you, is the first and initially the most important person to your achievement of the Individual Purpose. From birth, we instinctively possess what the Stoics called self-love, that which we call the drive for self-preservation and self-gratification. As we will discuss later, this drive is not a license for selfish and self-centred behaviour but merely an acceptance that you as an individual has value in and of itself. This instinct is to be seen as an indication that we are to place our own survival front and centre of our focuses. We are the starting point of life and the beginning of any endeavour. As such, we begin at Relational Proximity Level 1 (RP1), the closest level of proximity to the achievement of the purpose.

Once you reach maturity and select a suitable partner/spouse, the number of individuals at RP level 1 begins to increase. First, your spouse joins you at the highest level. Your spouse—male or female—occupies the position directly behind yourself in the RP level 1 hierarchy. This inclusion is recognition of their importance in the achievement of the purpose and the reciprocal duty owed between spouses. While at the same time recognising that as they are not carrying your genes, they are less critical to the achievement of the purpose than yourself or your offspring.

At this point, it is vital that we briefly touch on the most fundamental principle of the relationship between spouses. This principle is the mutual reciprocally of duties between spouses. This reciprocity means, in practice, that spouses take on mutual responsibility for the duties of each other. This expansion of duty is managed using the same principle as espoused in placing the spouse one down from the individual in question. You assume your spouse's duties, but they are always hierarchically slightly lower in priority than your own duties.

The most significant change occurs when you and your spouse have children. Up to this time, you have occupied pole position. Once your first child is born, you are demoted into second place as any parent will tell you. Having children is life-changing; once you have a child, your instinct for self-preservation becomes secondary to your instinct to ensure your child's survival. This reprioritisation is both natural and right and is more proof of the rightness of the purpose which we espouse.

The Individual Purpose is concerned with the continuation of life expressed in our case through the production and survival of children. Their survival is of paramount importance to the continuation of life, and as every parent knows, it is more important than their own individual survival. The below figure illustrates this changing hierarchy:

Prior to Children	After Children
1.1 You	1.1 Your First Child
1.2 Your Spouse	1.2 You
	1.3 Your Spouse

Figure 5: Prioritisation Before and After Children

When you and your spouse have subsequent children, you encounter the same prioritisation problem as before. How to prioritise between two individuals of equal value. If you were forced to prioritise between two or more of your children, how would you choose?

Ultimately, when we discuss prioritisation, we are talking about life or death decisions, such as the impossible question that parents face only too often, which child do you save when you can only save one? These are horrible situations that I hope we never face; however, any system cannot be a guide only in good times but must retain its validity in the worst of times. In the hardest of situations, we must remember the Individual Purpose and choose based on only two criteria. One, which person is, considering the facts known to you, most likely to survive and fulfil the purpose, and two, if this is undeterminable, we must prioritise the youngest individual.

The assumption implicit in prioritising the youngest individual where all else is equal is that youth equates to potential. Therefore, in differentiating between two individuals at the same Relational Proximity level in the same danger and with the same overall chances of survival, it is the youngest individual who should be considered to have the greatest proximity to the Purpose. This prioritisation of youth is an essential principle in Relational Proximity theory, forming a general rule for the prioritisation of individuals within RP levels. This principle is also consistent with the prioritisation of your children over yourself.

This process continues when your children have children of their own. Your grandchildren as the next generation of your offspring join the Relational Proximity level 1 with a nominal prioritisation based on their age. Your children's spouses also join RP1 but will assume the position directly behind that of your spouse. As with your spouse, by including your children's spouse in the highest level of the hierarchy of duty, it recognises their having joined your family and the duties resulting from this. While at the same time recognising that they are not of your blood and have only an ancillary role in the achievement of your purpose. On incorporating the preceding elements, we end up with the hierarchy below for a standard reproductive family:

Relational Proximity L1

1.1 Youngest Grandchild
1.2 Oldest Grandchild
1.3 Youngest Child
1.4 Oldest Child
1.5 You
1.6 Your Spouse
1.7 Your Childs Spouse

Relational Proximity (1)
Relational Proximity (2)
Relational Proximity (3)
Relational Proximity (4)

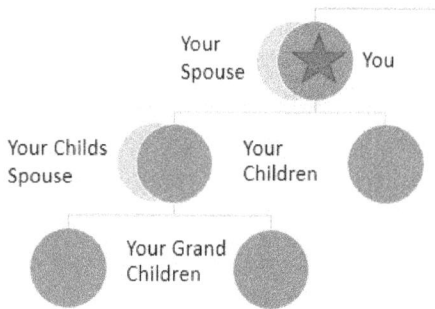

Your Spouse

You

Your Childs Spouse

Your Children

Your Grand Children

Figure 6: RP1 Graphical Representation

Relational Proximity Level 2: Family - Secondary Branch

The next Relational Proximity Level 2 (RP2) contains the secondary branches of your family. This branch includes both your birth family and that of your in-laws. The relative priority of each individual within this level is again determined by two criteria. One, which person is, considering the facts known to you, most likely to survive and fulfil the purpose, and two, if this is undeterminable, then the youngest individual is prioritised. This prioritisation results in a nominal hierarchy where your birth family is hierarchically placed one up from your spouse's birth family (your-in-laws).

This position is not to imply that all members of your birth family's secondary branches must be prioritised above all members of your spouse's siblings' families. Thus far, we have put forward the general principle that as youth generally equates to a potential to fulfil the Purpose, the younger individual typically has a closer proximity to the purpose than an older person. Hence, they have a higher priority in the hierarchy of duty. However, when we examine the prioritisation of persons outside of the primary family branch, the situation becomes more complicated. The reciprocally of duties between spouses, intended to assist both spouses in achieving the purpose, create a reciprocal union between the Individual Purpose of each spouse. As such, only differentiating individuals based on age is not enough. To solve this problem, we must consider the situation from the perspective of the Individual Purpose.

As the Individual Purpose is concerned with successful reproduction, it is evident that there must be a natural differentiation of people based on their reproductive fitness. In general, this divides people into four broad categories based on their age and reproductive fitness. The first category is Pre-Maturity, consisting of individuals from birth until they reach maturity at twenty years old. The second category is Maturity. This grouping consists of individuals who are reproductively able between the ages of twenty (20) to forty-five (45). This age corresponds in both men and women to the years of reproductive capability, after which reproduction is either impossible or highly problematic. The third grouping is Post-Maturity. This grouping consists of individuals who are not or are no longer reproductively able. This grouping consists of individuals older than forty-five (45) and those unfortunate individuals who are reproductively disabled. The final grouping is that of the Unfortunates. The Unfortunates membership is limited to those individuals who, through disability, are substantively unable to reproduce. Consistent with the principle of youth having priority, the Pre-Matures have the highest prioritisation, followed by the Matures, and finally, the Post-Matures.

Reproductive Categorisations	
Pre-Matures	0 - 20
Matures	20 - 45
Post-Matures	45-∞

Figure 7: Reproductive Categorisations

These categorisations make our problem of prioritisation between our siblings and your spouse's siblings much more straightforward, allowing us to effectively support the achievement of the Individual Purpose. In doing this, we first place each member of our families' secondary branches into the appropriate grouping with our spouse's family members just below our own. Once this is done, we can build our nominal hierarchy. To illustrate what is meant by this, let's consider the case where both you and your spouse have two siblings. Each of these siblings has a spouse of their own and two young children. The details of each individual are listed in the table below:

Your Siblings					Your Spouses Siblings			
Role	Age	Name	Age	Name	Age	Name	Age	Name
Sibling	46	Brian	28	Mazie	30	David	23	Jana
Spouse	39	Suzie	28	John	29	Hope	24	Robert
Child 1	18	Jack	5	Jim	8	Bob	3	Summer
Child 2	16	Jill	4	Jane	6	Kate	1	Hudson

Figure 8: RP2

Firstly, we place the Pre-Matures onto the list from youngest to oldest, starting with our blood relations and then our spouse's relations. Once this is done, we add the matures onto the list. We do this in the same way as with the pre-matures, placing blood relations on first, their spouses next, and then our spouse's relations. Finally, we add the Post-Matures on in the same way. One thing to note here is that spouses are always one position behind the relation. We can demonstrate this in that even though Suzie is a Mature and your brother Brian is a Post-mature, her priority is one below his. Once this is done, we end up with the following prioritisation list:

Pre-Matures		
Priority	**Age**	**Name**
2.1	4	Jane
2.2	5	Jim
2.3	16	Jill
2.4	18	Jack
2.5	1	Hudson
2.6	3	Summer
2.7	6	Kate
2.8	8	Bob
Matures		
2.9	28	Mazie
2.10	28	John
2.11	23	Jana
2.12	30	David
2.13	24	Robert
2.14	29	Hope
Post-Matures		
2.15	46	Brian
2.16	39	Suzie

Figure 9: RP2 Hierarchy

Relational Reliability

From RP Level 3 (RP3) onward, your obligation to an individual is based on a combination of their past actions and the considered probability of them assisting you and your family in the future. The quantification of these measures relies on the principles of Relational Reliability.

Relational Reliability refers to the balance of probabilities that a person will assist you and your family in the future. This is by necessity a speculative judgement, which, in practice, can only be approximated. This approximation is achieved by weighing an individual's history of reciprocity or Relational Obligation (RO) with your relative position in their Relational Proximity hierarchy or Relative Relational Proximity (RRP) to form a judgment of their future reliability. Relation Obligation is considered to be twice as meaningful as RRP in assessing future behaviour.

Relational obligation refers to the level of obligation which you fall under due to the past actions of an individual or group of individuals. It is based on the fundamental concept that our responsibilities to others are based largely on their past actions. We build relations with others in general by a process of sounding out their reliability by small tests of reciprocal actions. As a person proves their reliability to you and your family, their priority will increase as their role in assisting you in achieving your Individual Purpose increases.

The level of obligation implied can range from the mundane such as if a co-worker does you a small favour by buying you a coffee. Creating as a consequence a minor relational obligation which requires you to reciprocate by returning another small favour. To the far more substantial such as if a person saves your life or the life of one of your children. In this case, the relational obligation would be far more significant, creating an enduring obligation to that person and their family only one step below that of your siblings and their families. These obligations should not be understood as being transactional, whereby individuals return benefits received on a one for one basis. Instead, they should be seen as the links in the chains of reciprocity which bind us together as a community.

It is these chains of reciprocal obligation that are the difference between an individual who is part of your community and one who is not. The strength of these chains allows us to differentiate between an acquaintance and a friend, between a friend and those who are part of your 'family'. We create these chains by the offering and acceptance of obligations. For example, when you meet someone new, you may offer to buy them a drink. While you are physically offering a drink, you are offering much more. You are offering the person a chance to start a new relational obligation chain. You are signalling that you are interested in knowing them. Their acceptance creates an obligation between the two of you, which if they choose to reciprocate is the foundation for your future relationship. As we get to know the person, we make judgements about them, and if those judgements are favourable, we offer them more trust. If they accept the trust and reciprocate, our relationship will become stronger.

These trust levels can be quantified by assuming that there are five levels of relationships measured by RO; ranging from those who have shown themselves as able to be trusted to protect your children or who have saved your life in the past to those you have no previous obligations to. Each RO level is defined below:

Relational Obligation 1 (RP1) "Family":
This level of relational obligation consists of those who are part of your family, or who have saved your life or the life of someone in your reproductive family.

Relational Obligation 2 (RO2) "Friends":
This level is for those individuals who have provided consistent support to yourself and your family. Generally, those we consider close friends.

Relational Obligation 3 (RO3) "Community":
This level is the default level in which all members of your community sit.

RO4 "Allies":
RO4 is where all those people to whom you share a level of mutual responsibility sit. This level includes workmates, members of friendly communities, fellow passengers, and everyone else whom you know personally but who do not fit into any of the higher groupings.

RO5 "Outsiders":
This level connotes those individuals who are unknown to you, belong to non-friendly communities, or otherwise have

no prior relationship with you. This level is the default level for all beings not otherwise categorised.

In this way, at RP level 3 and below, a person's RP is based mainly on their past actions. Implicit in this is the expectation that an individual's past actions are positively correlated with the probability of their future actions. We expect that if a person has previously fulfilled their duties to us, they are likely to do so in the future. However, as past behaviour is only partially indicative of future actions in similar circumstances, we must be cautious. There is always uncertainty in what a person may do in the future, and we must never forget that, like us, they have responsibilities to those higher in their RP hierarchy, which must come first.

This mutual prioritisation is factored into the RP hierarchy by recognising that everyone prioritises people who sit higher in their RP hierarchy in the same way as we do. The implication of this is that the higher we sit in an individual's RP hierarchy, the more likely we are to be prioritised compared to others. The more likely we are to be prioritised, the more likely they are to assist us in a crisis. For clarity, this is defined as Relative Relational Proximity (RRP). This outcome is logical if we consider that the lower an individual's RP level is, the more people come before them in a crisis.

RRP can be conceptualised by understanding that the RRP and RP are fundamentally the same but from a different viewpoint. RP is where people relate to you, and RRP is where you sit on a person's RP hierarchy. For clarity's sake, anyone who is not a RP 1 or 2 receives a nominal RRP value of 3.

We can demonstrate this by comparing the position of one of your siblings to that of your child. In a crisis, your child's survival comes first as they are an RP1, your sibling comes second as an RP2. This precept means that if only one of the two can survive, your sibling would be left to die. From your sibling's view, this would be clear as well. He would know that your child and you would come first in your RP hierarchy as you both have RRPs of 1 while he has an RRP of 2. Just as you would know to him, he would come first as his RRP to himself is RRP1, followed by your child and then yourself as RRP 2s.

We use these two figures to calculate our Relational reliability, which equates directly with the individuals RP level. This calculation is done by multiplying the Relational Obligation value by 2 (to account for its greater reliability) and then adding the Relative Relation Obligation. The equation used is below:

$$RP \geq 3 = RR = ((RO * 2) + RRP)$$

Figure 10: Relation Reliability

By expanding this with all RO levels from 1-5 and with all RRP levels, we get a table of results as illustrated below:

RO					
	1	2	3	4	5
R 1	3	5	7	9	11
R 2	4	6	8	10	12
P 3	5	7	9	11	13

Figure 11: RO vs. RRP = RR

To explain this concept further, we will now describe the process using a few examples. Your parents and grandparents generally occupy the pinnacle of the relationships defined by reciprocal altruism, RP3. This relationship is defined as are all others based on the Relational reliability metrics of Relational Obligation (RO) and Relative Relational Proximity (RRP). In most cases, your parents' claim to superior RO status has been established through their actions throughout your childhood.

In this period of your life, your survival was dependant on your parents in every respect. It can safely be assumed that they have saved your life many times over. They have fed you, clothed you, educated you, protected you, etc. Your whole existence is owed to them, which can be objectively seen to have created the most profound relational obligation possible. These past actions would place them squarely at RO1. Next, we consider our RRP.

Your position in their RP hierarchy is RP1 as their purpose runs through to you directly in the same way as it does to your children. This results in an RRP1 ranking, placing you and your family ahead of virtually all other considerations for your parents. Next, to calculate their RP level, we add two times the RO level with the RRP level. In this case, it would result in an RR of 3 or an RP level of RP3 ((RO1)*2+(RRP1)=3)

If, however, your grandparents had not played a significant part in your life or perhaps one of your parents had been absent from your life, the result would be different. The process followed would be the same. You would first determine what level of RO existed between yourself and the individual in question. Let us assume that, in this instance, they had been entirely absent from your life and are not members of your community, resulting in a RO of 4. Your RRP would still not have changed as you are still their grandchild with an RP to them of 1. This results in an RRP of 1. Calculating this, you get an RP level of 9 (4*2+1=9).

From here, the process of prioritisation follows the same method as that expressed in RP2. The individuals are broken into the various groupings based on reproductive maturity and sorted internally by age. Blood family again comes first, followed by stepparents, and then in-laws. Below is a nominal hierarchy of priority at RP3 for a standard family consisting of you and your spouse's parents and grandparents:

Matures		
Priority	**Age**	**Name**
3.1	41	Parent 2 (blood)
3.2	42	Parent 1 (blood)
3.3	39	Parent 1
3.4	41	Parent 2
Post-Matures		
3.5	63	Maternal Grandparent 2 (blood)
3.6	65	Paternal Grandparent 2 (blood)
3.7	67	Maternal Grandparent 1 (blood)
3.8	68	Paternal Grandparent 1 (blood)
3.9	63	Paternal Grandparent 2
3.10	65	Paternal Grandparent 1
3.11	68	Maternal Grandparent 1
3.12	71	Maternal Grandparent 2

Figure 12: RR Example 1

This process can again be demonstrated using any other individual. Let us take a non-related friend as an example. We will assume that they have built a good relationship with you having exchanged favours and obligations over a couple of years. This relationship you rate as being an RO2 level relationship (close friendship). As you are not in their reproductive chain, you will have an RRP of 3. If we calculate this out, we can find their relative RR. RO2 times two equals four added to RRP3 results in an RP of seven. Again, if you have multiple people at RR7, the standard prioritisation process will provide you with a nominal hierarchy. This nominal hierarchy is, as described previously, ordered by common-sense, maturity classification, blood relationship, and age.

The last part of Relational Reliability, which we have not yet discussed, is how it is related to the reproductive families of those persons who are part of your Relational Proximity hierarchy. From RP3 onwards, everyone occupies a position related to their past actions in support of you or your family's survival. It is logical as we all aim after our families' long-term survival that the support provided by other people should be reciprocated. We achieve this by placing all persons with an RP of 1 with an individual in your hierarchy at the same level as those in your RP hierarchy when no other relationship exists. This means that if your friend has an RR/RP level of 7, their spouse, children, and grandchildren will also become RP7s. If you develop a relationship with any of these individuals, they will maintain their reflected RP while it is higher than their (earned) RP value. This process creates a clear requirement for friends and community members to protect each other's families prioritised by their RR/RP levels while also allowing them to develop relationships with friends and acquaintance's family members.

For added clarity, the table below illustrates this by showing the relative ranking of a diverse set of individuals at RR7:

Pre-Matures		
Priority	Age	Name
7.1	5	Cousin (blood)
7.2	6	Cousin (blood)
7.3	5	Cousin (Marriage)
Matures		
7.4	35	Cousin (blood)
7.5	21	Friend
Post-Matures		
7.6	50	Cousin (blood)
7.7	47	Cousin (Marriage)
7.8	46	Friend

Figure 13: Example

This hierarchical structure allows us to place all individuals into a clear hierarchy of priority quickly, allowing us to prioritise between individuals easily at all times. However, there is one further prioritisation mechanism required. So far, we have discussed prioritisation between individuals. However, one other complication occurs when there are groups involved. With internally homogenous groups, we utilise the RP mechanism choosing the groups that have the highest RP level as we did with individuals. This mechanism also works when the groups are internally heterogeneous, again, we choose the group which has the individual with the highest RP in it. This mechanism breaks down when we are faced with choosing between two or more groups that consist of individuals with the same RP level.

Prioritising between Groups

In this case, Relational Proximity cannot help you prioritise between them. To better illustrate and aid in conceptualising the problem, we will introduce the trolley problem as introduced by Frank Chapman Sharp and or Philippa Foot. In the original form of this thought experiment, you are placed in the position of 'driver of a runaway tram which can only be steered from one narrow track on to another; five men are working on one track and one man on the other; anyone on the track you enter is bound to be killed'. For our purposes, each of the men have the same RP as each other. Which way do we turn?

To answer this question, we need to consider the problem from the perspective of the purpose of life. In this case, each person is of equal value to us in achieving our Individual Purpose. To decide, we need to determine their potential. We used age to approximate this earlier, yet it does not work here. This is because not only are the ages of the individuals unlikely to be known to us in real life, but it is not apparent how one would estimate the potential of a group without the use of mathematical formulations, which would prove themselves to be unviable in the cut and thrust of life. Instead, we will satisfice as we did with age by saying that if we must choose between harming two groups with the same RP level, we should choose the option that will result in the least harm. In this case, by steering onto the track with the single man on it, not the one with five men.

This solution solves this dilemma, but as any of you familiar with the trolley problem would have recognised, there are several other versions of the problem that need to be examined. The next problem is the related 'fat man problem'. 'As before, a trolley is hurtling down a track towards five people. You are on a bridge under which it will pass, and you can stop it by putting something very heavy in front of it. As it happens, there is a very fat man next to you – your only way to stop the trolley is to push him over the bridge and onto the track, killing him to save five. Should you push him?' Again, we will assume that all involved individuals are at the same RP level.

At first glance, the problem looks to be the same as the tradi-tional trolley problem; however, it is not. The core difference is that the fat man is not in danger while the single man on the track is due to his location. To advocate for the fat man's killing is to implicitly allow for unbridled expansion of risk, which will make none of us ever safe. This problem becomes more evident in the derivative of this problem developed by Judith Jarvis Thomson, coined the 'Transplant thought experiment'.

In this experiment, 'A transplant surgeon has five patients, each in need of a different organ, each of whom will die without that organ. Unfortunately, there are no organs available to perform any of these five transplant operations. A healthy young traveller, just passing through the city the doctor works in, comes in for a routine check-up. In the course of doing the check-up, the doctor discovers that his organs are compatible with all five of his dying patients. Suppose further that if the young man were to disappear, no one would suspect the doctor. Do you support the morality of the doctor to kill that tourist and provide his healthy organs to those five dying people and save their lives?' If the same assumptions apply as with the fat man experiment, you will perhaps see more viscerally the danger of equating the fat man with the worker on the line.

The difference comes down to the potentiality of the event. In the case of the workers on the line, all six persons are in danger due to the potentiality of a runaway trolley while working on a track and the dichotomy of the switch. In the case of the fat man and the traveller, the potentiality does not exist or at least does not exist without your direct action. Without your direct action, there is no chance of the fat man being pushed in front of the trolley just as there is no potentiality of a standard medical check-up being fatal. To allow for potentiality to be expanded would result in a situation whereby nowhere is safe, compromising the achievement of the purpose.

By this, we mean that if we expand potentiality from the situation to the wider world, we effectively create a situation where we are, at all times, in danger of being sacrificed from some apparent greater good. By limiting ourselves to those at risk from the potentialities of the event, we allow ourselves to prioritise where a choice must be made, while at the same time, preventing undesirable externalities. We will discuss the morality of these choices in the next chapter.

18

Perspectivism and Morality

"Whatever moral rules you have deliberately proposed to yourself. abide by them as if they were laws,
and as if you would be guilty of impiety by violating
any of them. Don't regard what anyone says of you,
for this, after all, is no concern of yours."

Epictetus, the Enchiridion

The morality in this system stems from the Purpose being
fundamentally consequentialist. An act is right or wrong only
if it promotes or harms your Individual Purpose's achievement,
namely the long-term welfare of your family. This results in a
stern morality stripped of all feel-good platitudes and pleasant
lies. Depending on the situation, it requires and justifies great
acts of kindness, humility, and self-sacrifice as well as acts
of almost inhuman viciousness. The end always justifies the
means for the end is nothing more than the survival of the
species through your family's survival.

However, this is not a blank check allowing us to do whatever we like. Instead, it is a robust morality that demands that we examine each of our actions to see if it promotes our purpose. It requires a level of introspection in each of us, as we ask how each action will affect our families our communities and ultimately each living thing. It must be emphasised that this is not a morality that gels with the Judaeo-Christian morals many of us have grown up with. While many of the actions that support your family's or community's survival indeed resonate with the Christian ideals at times, the logic of alignment with the Purpose leads to actions as being right, which would be considered evil under Christianity and vice versa.

The morality of the Code rests on the pillar of 'Perspectivism'. Perspectivism is a system of ethics which places the achievement of the Individual Purpose of the being at the foremost of moral consideration. In its simplest form, it can be expressed as meaning that an act which contributes positively to the achievement of the Individual Purpose by either supporting the family, community or your own survival is 'good'. In contrast, those acts which impede the achievement of your Individual Purpose or harm your families, communities or own survival are 'bad'. What is essential to recognise in the conception of Perspectivism is that the act's morality is entirely based on the individual. An act can be right if it enhances the achievement of the individual's IP even if it harms another being. It judges the intended consequence of the act on the individual, their kin, and their community as being of greater importance than the effect on the others.

As every living thing has an equal value at the universal level with the relative value being entirely dependent on the subject and the achievement of their IP, every being is engaged in a kind of Hobbesian 'war of all against all'. This results in the continuation of existence often being predicated on the destruction of other beings. This reality is apparent when we consider that each breath we take, every morsel of food we eat, and every movement we make results in harm to countless other beings. This harm is undoubtedly an evil to those who are harmed, yet as it is necessary for our survival and, by extension, the achievement of our purpose, it is a good to us. This duality of effect is unavoidable in any moral decision where a choice must be made between harming another or being harmed oneself. To the one harmed, the act was an evil, yet to the one not harmed, the act was a good. We can only reconcile this duality of harm if we recognise that morality is predicated on perspective.

This focus on the perspective of the subject is an accounting of the fact that morality is anchored to the subject actor's perspective. This Perspectivism means that what is good is good because, from the standpoint of the agent, the act will or is at least likely to promote the achievement of their Individual Purpose. Conversely, what is bad is bad as it harms the agent's achievement of their Individual Purpose. An example of this is when a wolf hunts and kills a deer. The wolf kills to eat and survive or feed its pack so that they may survive, and by extension, it may achieve its Individual Purpose. This act is right from the wolf's perspective, irrespective of the consequence on the deer or the deer's Individual Purpose.

In the same way, if your child was freezing to death, it would be 'right' to take a blanket from another person even if this would lead to that individual's death. The act would be 'right' as it promoted your child's survival and thus, the achievement of your Individual Purpose even though it resulted in the death of another human being. In both cases, the being harmed would suffer evil from their perspective, but the other would possess a good.

Perspectivism sits on the foundation of the unity of the value of life, recognising at once that all living things have equal value and that the universal nature is one of conflict between individual organisms. This understanding of the universal nature requires an acceptance that the survival of one individual often requires the death of another. This necessity is not wrong but is merely a fundamental element of the nature of existence. It is the duty of all individuals to strive for continued existence. An acceptance of this reality should not lead to a fatalistic resignation but to a striving for life.

All living things are compelled by the purpose of life in the same way we are. When we kill a living thing to survive, we do good in so far as it contributes to the achievement of our Individual Purpose by aiding the survival of ourselves, our families, or our communities. In the same way, when we prevent ourselves and our own from being harmed, we also do right. However, in addition to this, we recognise that other beings are driven by the same impulse as us. Therefore, we accept that in the same circumstances as we would be right to harm another, the other would be right to harm us.

We may best explain this through an analogy. The grass seeks after its survival and the continuation of its species in the same way as all living things. In the pursuit of its Individual Purpose, it will, through its automatic cellular defences, kill many micro-organisms, which, in pursuing their own continued existence, could harm it. The grass does not consider the aims or interests of the things it kills any more than the micro-organisms consider the interests of the grass. It kills without thought to survive and reproduce. But what of the animals who eat the grass to survive?

Let us take a sheep for example. A sheep survives and achieves its Individual Purpose by eating and, in some cases, killing grasses and other plants. It does this without considering the plant's welfare any more than it considers the micro-organisms that are killed by its hoofs or immune system. It acts merely as necessary to survive and reproduce and does right consequently even though this action results in the death of a multitude of living beings.

The sheep may then be preyed on by other animals who kill to survive and reproduce just as the sheep and the grass did. This circle of harm is right. The inherent equality of value of each individual being from its perspective, coupled with the innate drive to achieve the purpose of life, justifies survival. If it is necessary to kill any living thing, including a fellow human to survive or protect those we are bound to protect, then it is right to do so. This rationale is as valid if the person is attacking you or yours or is simply in possession of an object that is essential to your or your family's survival. It is the agent's perspective that defines the right action, not the perspective of the other. This precept is not to be taken to mean that perspectivist morality promotes action without consideration for the effect on others.

Quite the opposite, Perspectivism is intimately concerned with the consequences of actions. To act without consideration for the likely reaction of other beings or the long-term effect of the action would be to act recklessly. While being entirely focused on the welfare of the individual, Perspectivism will, through the enlightened self-interest of the adherent, lead inexorably to the increased welfare of their family, kin, community, and all other sentient beings.

This outcome is indeed the only one that can germinate from the soil of Perspectivism if adequately understood. As any person whom the conception takes root in will find themselves unable to act otherwise as they will realise that their selfish interests are served by acting in the 'good' way and are harmed in acting in the 'bad' way. To explain this, we must understand the consequences of our acts. To determine if an act harms or helps, it is not enough to only look at the immediate effect. It is necessary to look at the broader long-term effects as well.

It also helps if we consider our proposed actions to be normative in nature, which means that we assume that the propositional right action will be the default action taken by all people in society. Therefore, an action must be consistently right, i.e. in all similar circumstances, no matter the moral actor or the victim, the action must remain correct. In this way, if you are right to harm a being (animal or plant) to eat it or use its by-products, another being must be right to harm you for similar reasons. If you are right to lie to protect yourself, then another is right to lie. If you are right to steal, then another is right to steal in similar circumstances, and so on. When dealing with non-sentient beings, this is mostly academic. If we harm one or not is primarily dependent on our want.

The non-sentient being's existence is, to us, primarily one of expediency. If harming it will benefit us, we will harm it. If preserving it benefits us, we should preserve it. As the non-sentient lack the ability to do us harm, except in the moment, we naturally consider them as 'resources' for want of a better term. We should use them for our benefit, recognising that if our positions were reversed, then they should do the same to us if it would benefit them. This conclusion is not to be seen to be an argument for unsustainable exploitation. Unsustainable exploitation is self-defeating for even if you personally benefit, eliminating the resource will harm your community and or family in the long run.

With sentient beings who will be referred to as 'persons' from here on, the situation is different. The difference is not with their inherent value (which is not different) but merely in their potential to repay the harm done to them. This potentiality is what makes it generally wrong to harm them. Humans are the only species we know of thus far which can be referred to as a sentient as we mean it here. Their sentience gives them this enhanced harm potential. They both collectively and individually remember the harm that is done to them and can repay that harm at a later date. When you consider the consequences of harming a human, you will quickly perceive that risks exist, which do not with the non-sentient being. If you injure a person, they, their kin, or community members are highly likely to seek revenge. This potential makes the potential for harming them to result to harm to you, your family, or your community much greater than it does with non-sentient beings. The risk is so significant that there is only one situation where the gain outweighs the potential harm, making it right to harm them. That being any situation where not to harm them would result in greater harm to yourself, your family, or your community.

Further to this is the relation of the individual and their family to the community. The community exists to support the individuals and their families, which make up the community. The individual citizens join in the community for the benefits of mutual protection and the pooling of resources and skills to promote their Individual Purposes' collective achievement. The corollary of this pooling of resources and security is that an attack on one citizen must, by necessity, be an attack on all. This mutual obligation creates a reciprocal form of collective morality within a community whereby citizens and visitors refrain from harming other individuals due to the implicit threat of retribution by the whole. This collective retribution is the basis for all law. If someone harms my family or me, then the community must revenge me. In the same way, if I harm my community, then the other members are obliged to revenge themselves upon me.

A good action would therefore be one that both contributes positively to your family's welfare and contributes to or at least does not harm the community's welfare. A bad action, there-fore, would be one that harms your family's or community's welfare. At this point, it is worth clarifying the term harm and harming.

Harming means any action that damages an individual's achievement of their Individual Purpose. Generally, an individual can be harmed in three main ways: physically, through deception, and through theft.

Physical Harm

An individual can be physically harmed in several different ways. You can harm someone by physically attacking them. Or by not acting when you could to prevent them from being physically harmed. You can harm someone by withholding food, clothing, or shelter from them when to do so would lead to them being harmed. You can harm someone by using communication or lack of communication to cause them to harm themselves. The consequence of each of these actions is the same in that, through conscious action or inaction, a being is physically harmed. The consciousness of the harm being caused is important. To harm without knowledge is not a matter of morality but instead of law. For us, it is sufficient to say that once an individual becomes aware of the harm they are causing, they are bound by the moral law to prevent it unless compelled by duty to their family, community, or self to inflict it.

Physical harm by its very nature hinders the being's achievement of their Individual Purpose. Of course, how much harm is done depends on the severity of the injury done to them. To be clear, when we talk of harm, we are not talking about the infliction of pain. We are talking of an injury that prevents an individual from permanently or temporally carrying out their duties to their kin or community. Why this is a wrong can be seen from the flow of harm, which harm to an individual entails.

When an individual is physically harmed, the injury is not limited to them alone, it flows to their family and their community. Take a young person whom, in some personal dispute, is killed. The first to suffer are their reproductive family (their children and spouse) if they have them. They lose a provider and a protector, reducing their chances of survival. They lose the individual's knowledge and support; they lose everything they could have been to them. In short, their chances of achieving their Individual Purposes are reduced.

Next, their birth and family-in-law are harmed as their death prevents further children from being produced. By preventing them from assisting his brothers or sisters or nephews and nieces, the physical harm done to them reduces the chances for the family to survive and achieve its purpose. Next, their community is also harmed.

Their death removes the individual from the community, weakening it through the loss of their productive efforts, removing their ability to protect or contribute to the community and diminishing it by their loss. The community loses any benefit the person may have provided in the future. In this way, the harm done to one member of a community affects the whole.

This harm is amplified further if considered as a categorical imperative. If everyone in a community was to, at whim, inflict harm on others, we must ask what the consequences would be to any one individuals' survival. The consequences of unrestrained violence or the rule of the strong over the weak is tyranny. The strong do as they will, and the weak suffer what they must to borrow a line from Thucydides. To judge the pernicious effect of this anarchy, we need only look to those areas of the globe where there are civil war and disorder. In every case, we can see a strong correlation with disorder and want.

The more prevalent violence is in a community, the greater the risk is involved in all activities. The greater the danger, the greater the share of total productive resources which must be directed into security instead of productivity. We can see this instability premium if we look at the cost of doing business around the world. In areas where violence is common, business costs are greater compared with similar low violence countries. It can, again, be seen in the size of military expenditures by nations, as the risk of conflict increases the percentage of the nation's productive capacity, which is expended on security can be reliably seen to increase. We can even see this insecurity premium at the micro-level. As individuals, we start to spend more of our own resources on alarms, cameras, and security barriers as the perceived risk of crime increases in our area. As we can see, violence or the infliction of physical harm on persons (sentient-beings) is generally harmful, it behoves us to restrain ourselves unless the consequence of not acting is that harm would be done to our community, our families, or ourselves.

Harm Through Theft

Another way in which we can be harmed is through the theft of our property. Before discussing this form of harm, we must define what we mean by both the terms theft and property. Property is defined as the rights possessed by an individual to the benefits and or use of a thing or being. In this conception, an individual's ownership of something or being is, in essence, the mutual recognition by members of a community of the terms under which a person may enjoy the benefits of said item. What those terms are is a matter for the community. However, in most societies that I am aware of, there is at least a nominal relationship between the production of one's body and ownership. It is to be understood as both the fruit of items and labour. If I possess a plot of land, then my property is the fruits of that land as defined in my community. If I use my body, which I own, to produce something, then I own the fruits of that labour either in whole or in part. If you take my labour and then withhold payment, then you steal from me as surely as if you stole an object from me.

Theft is, therefore, the prevention of the rightful enjoyment of property rights to the detriment of the rightful owner. This definition is sufficiently robust to cover the enjoyment of someone's property in a manner that does not cause detriment to the owner such as hiking through it, sitting on a seat or stoop set outside one's residence, or making use of abandoned clothing or structures. While, at the same time, establishing a sufficiently high bar for the protection of property.

Theft is a form of harm as it harms an individual's achievement of their purpose through depriving them of resources by which they would provide for their family and support their community. This is as true of the theft of a pin as for the theft of a person's life savings. In each case, the affected individual has been harmed, though the severity differs. The true effect of theft is similar to the impact of personal harm in that it makes survival harder. In the case of physical violence, it is the use of their body that the individual is deprived of. In the case of theft, it is the individual's property or the production of their body which they are deprived of. In both cases, the effect is to increase the cost of production of any item reducing supply, increasing want and making survival harder.

If you were a farmer, would you invest in expensive farming machines or other productivity improvements if you were likely to have them stolen? Would you build for the long-term if you could be thrown off the land at any time? Theft is pernicious in that it takes from the productive and gives to the unproductive.

Again, consider the effects of theft on both the individual and the community. Suppose if theft were carried to the natural extreme and became universal. With widespread theft, I could not be sure of the enjoyment of my property or of the payment for my labour. If I grow food, I cannot be sure that I will be able to use it to feed my family. If I work for another, I cannot be sure that they will pay me for my labour. This uncertainty makes it much more challenging to survive and disincentivise investment in or work for the future.

This harm to the achievement of the IP is the argument against theft except, as with physical harm, if the consequence of not acting is that harm would be done to our community, our families, or ourselves. By not stealing, except in these circumstances, we can help enhance the achievement of our own Individual Purpose and positively contribute to the commonweal.

Harming Though Deceit

The third form of harm is that done through deceit. Deceit is a cousin to the first forms of harm, often accompanying or preceding them. Deceit harms through leading others to make decisions which are against their interests. Deceit harms by requiring the imposition of protection against deception. These can take the form of simply the loss of productive time as individuals are forced to spend time to confirm the veracity of information. It can take the form of loss of productive potential as resources are used to create procedural or legal protections against deceit. It can take the form of lost opportunities as the potential for deception increases the risk of investments, the cost of doing business, and reduces the incentive to collaborate with others. If taken to an extreme, it leads to civil strife as we become uncertain about who can be trusted, damaging social cohesion and the rule of law.

It is not hard to see the harmful effects of deceit in any community. We need only to look around at our own lives. We can see the benefits that accrue to those who are trusted, and conversely, the disadvantage and the opprobrium, which affects those who are not. We feel the frustration of the time wasted as we wade through contracts trying to see if there is some deceit when we get work done or take a new job. We feel the sting when the deceitful pull the wool over our eyes. We feel frustrated when that guy at work leaves the work for us to do and deceives the bosses about how busy he has been. We are frustrated by politicians who mortgage the truth for their careers.

Deceit is pernicious and harmful in a family and a community. It seduces us into taking the easy path by allowing us to hide behind lies. It excuses us in our failures with the idea that we can hide them from others. It makes every decision harder—every assessment chancier. Deceit is like a fire lit in a forest. It seems like a good idea until it grows out of control.

19

A Framework for Moral Decision-Making

"A man does what he must - in spite of personal consequences, in spite of obstacles and dangers and pressures - and that is the basis of all human morality."
  John F. Kennedy

If morality is situation-dependent, then we must have a framework to support moral decision-making. To build this framework, we must synthesise all the previous elements into a mental system, which can allow for quick decision-making in all the possible situations that we could face. This framework consists of asking three questions that can lead to three outcomes. The three questions we should always ask ourselves before acting are: one, will this decision have a positive, neutral, or negative effect on my family or self (RP1 to 3)? Two, will this decision have a negative impact on my community (RP 3+)? Three, is it essential that I do this? After considering the three questions in order, you will know if you should do it, if you can do it or not as per your whim, or if you should not do it.

Question one serves to help focus your mind on the core of the purpose, namely your family's survival. By seeking to understand the consequences of the decision on these most vital persons, you can better know if you should act. If the consequences of the decision are negative, skip to question three as the effect on your community can be ignored. However, if the consequences on your family are either positive or neutral, you should go on to question two. Once you have determined what effect the proposed action will have on your family (RP1 to 3), you must consider if the proposed action will harm your community.

This concern for the impact of our decisions on our community forms the second question we must answer prior to acting. This question is important as our community is a major contributor to our achievement of the purpose. By harming them, by extension, we harm ourselves. If the proposed decision will not harm them, and if the effect on ourselves or our families are positive, we should act. If the effect is neutral, then it is up to your inclination to act or not act. However, if the decision's effects will harm our community, we have to ask one more question before we know how we should act.

Question three is "is this act essential?". This question needs only to be asked if the foreseen outcome is either negative to yourself, your family, or your community. The essence of this question is the concept that the means justifies the end of achievement of the purpose. It is essential to physically harm, steal, or deceive to ensure your or your family's survival; then it is moral to do so in that circumstance. Question three serves to act as a slow point in the decision-making process. Asking those confronted by it to carefully reflect if the action they are contemplating is absolutely essential. If there is another way to achieve the purpose that will not result in as negative an outcome, you must do that instead.

If one determines that the proposed act is indeed essential, then they should act. However, they should also be willing to accept the negative consequences which will follow. Have no illusion that while the 'essential' decision is morally right, it remains a choice between two evils. We must accept that the ethically right choice is often simply the choice which does the least harm. This willingness to do necessary evil is where Code varies markedly from the mainstream Judeo-Christian morality as espoused in the ten commandments or Kant's deontological ethics, both of whom place the act ahead of the consequence.

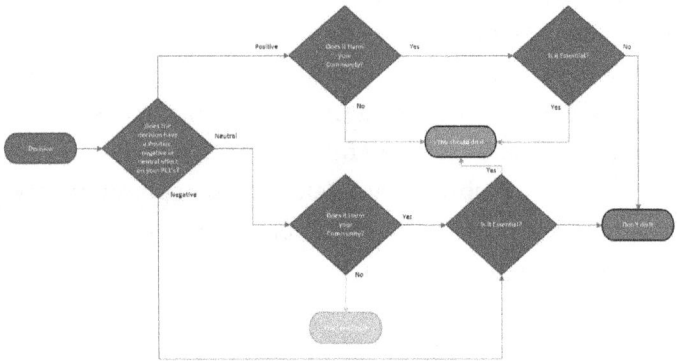

Figure 14: The Framework for Moral Decision Making

To understand this framework better and to see how to implement it in practice, it will be useful to work through some
illustrative examples to see how this system works.

Example 1: Kill or be Killed

The first scenario is relatively simple. While walking in the
forest with another person, you are confronted by an armed
individual. The person tells you that you must choose either
yourself or the other person to be killed. He informs you that if
you fail to choose, he will kill both of you. To decide, you ask
the three questions.

**Will this decision have a positive, neutral, or negative effect
on my family or self (PL1-3)?**

In this case, what we are asking boils down to who the other person is. If they have a higher Relational Proximity than yourself, i.e. if they are one of your kids, then it will harm your family (RP1-3). If they don't have a higher Relational Proximity, then choosing them will positively affect your family as you will be alive. In this instance, there is no neutral choice possible. If the decision will harm yourself or your family, you go to question three, if not, you proceed to question two.

Will this decision have a negative effect on my community (PL3+)?

There is only one possibility in this circumstance: by choosing the other person, you will harm your community. As such, we move on to question three.

Is this act essential?

In this scenario, we can be confident that it is essential that we choose as not to choose will result in the worst outcome. Therefore, we know we should choose either ourselves or the other person to be killed. To determine which choice is morally correct, we rely on the prioritisation rules set out earlier. The person with the lowest Relational Proximity score must be chosen for death even if that person is you.

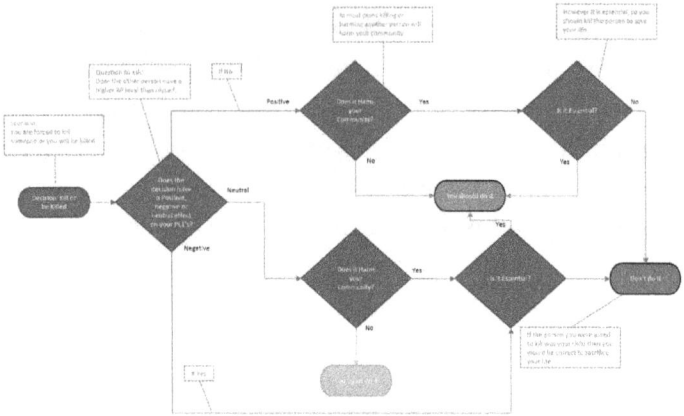

Figure 15: Kill or be Killed

Example 2: The Trolley Problem

For our second example, let us look at a more complex scenario. As introduced by Frank Chapman Sharp and or Philippa Foot, the Trolley Problem is the basis of the second example. We have already examined this scenario in the Prioritisation section; however, for clarity's sake, let us return to it and use the three questions to determine the morally correct action. In the original form of this thought experiment, you are placed in the position of 'driver of a runaway tram which can only be steered from one narrow track on to another; five men are working on one track and one man on the other; anyone on the track you enter is bound to be killed'. In this scenario, it is assumed that you must choose one or the other track. Which track do we choose? We begin again by asking the first question.

Will this decision have a positive, neutral, or negative effect on my family or self (PL1-3)?

In the context of the trolley problem, we are really asking if anyone on either track is a member of our family (RP1-3). If there is a family member (RP1-3) on one or more tracks, then the consequence of the decision on our families will be negative. If there is not a member of our family on either track, the consequences will be neutral. If the consequences are negative, as always, we skip to question three. If the consequences are neutral, we will proceed to question two.

Will this decision have a negative effect on my community (PL3+)?

In the trolley problem, as whatever choice you make, you will harm a person and you will necessarily harm your community. As such, we move on to the third question.

Is this act essential?

In the trolley problem, we are again faced with a choice of two evils. Either option will harm someone, so we must choose one of the tracks, and therefore, we must harm either the single worker or the five workers. Again, if we are here, we will rely on the prioritisation rules to determine the morally correct action. In this scenario, if we assume that the workers have the same Relational Proximity to us, we will choose to steer on the track with only one worker. This decision will be predicated on the greater potential which the five workers have to contribute to our IP achievement compared to the single worker.

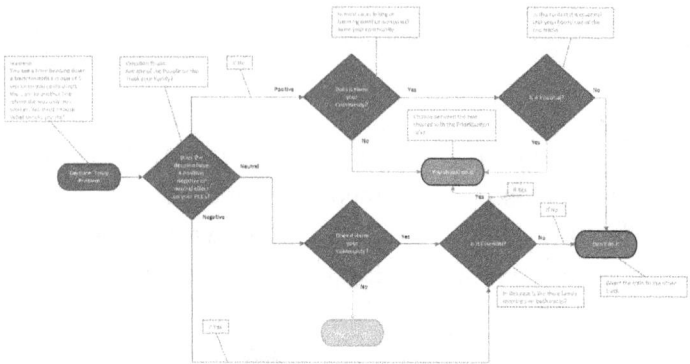

Figure 16: Trolley Problem

Example 3: Gambling

Let us now move to a more mundane problem. Gambling is a popular recreation for many people; however, it is a crippling addiction for some. Using the moral decision framework, let us examine gambling and its morality. Gambling is defined by the Encyclopedia Britannica as "The betting or staking of something of value, with consciousness of risk and hope of gain, on the outcome of a game, a contest, or an uncertain event whose result may be determined by chance or accident". We are here going to talk specifically about the wagering on games of chance.

Unlike in the previous examples where the decisions were absolutes, in the case of gambling and many other things, it is not possible to provide an absolute answer. In broad terms, every decision we make is a gamble. The world is governed by chance and fortune; therefore, there is always the risk of loss. In the specific case of the gambling of money on games of chance or uncertain events, it comes down to a judgement of the threshold for when harm is done.

If you are physically harming people, stealing, or lying to continue to gamble, you are obviously exceeding this threshold. However, it can be hard to determine in practice. As a rule of thumb, it is useful to practice openness and honesty if you choose to engage in potentially addictive behaviours. If you want to gamble, then by all means bet but be sure that you are open about it. Consider as your guide that if you are unwilling to tell your spouse or parents about your gambling, then it is inadvisable to place the bet.

It may be useful to consider your aim in gambling. Ask yourself: to what purpose am I placing this bet? If it is for recreation, then set the same limits on it as you would for all other enter- tainments. Place it last among your priorities as if befitting a luxury. This is more proper in relation to betting at a particular and occasional event where the entertainment consists of the game of chance such as at a casino or a horse racing circuit and is not principally concerned with financial gain.

If your aim in placing a bet is financial gain, then great caution should be exercised. Games of chance, as the old adage says, are designed so that 'The house always wins'. Your chances of receiving a positive financial return, in the long run, are long and the temptation to chase your losses are high. Indeed, while all gambling can increase the risk of developing harmful behaviours, gambling motivated by greed carries the most significant risk.

Consider gambling as a recreational activity if you wish to do it. Set a small amount you can afford to spend as your limit and give your word to someone else not to breach it. This stratagem has the benefit of prompting sober judgment of the amount you wish to spend and placing the barrier of your word in the way of the temptation to chase your losses. If, however, these strategies fail to check your gaming carefully, consider your actions because you are likely heading towards harming your family or community, which is a breach of our duty.

With the elucidation of the framework for moral decision-making, we come to the end of this work's third book. At this point, we have built what is hopefully a compelling and logically consistent system which should allow us to live our lives with purpose and with the confidence that comes from the knowledge of the correctness of our actions. In book one, we deduced the nature of reality as is presented to our senses as being one governed by causation, both explicit (calculable effect) and implicit (chance/fortune). With objects divided into two classes, those with independent agency (life), which we called beings, and those without, which we termed things.

From here, we inferred from the inherent sameness between beings that the purpose of life is to continue with the various divisions of beings (classes of species, species, individuals) seeking after this ultimate purpose in their unique manner. From this realisation, it followed that we as beings shared this purpose.

In book two, we examined how humans achieved this purpose, discussing the role, nature, and duties to the self, family, and community. In book three. we explored the conflicts that could occur between the duties which we had examined and presented the ethical system of our Code. This system consisted of a hierarchical system of prioritisation and a framework for moral decision-making. What is left now is to place what we have discovered into practice. Examining the various elements of human society from our system's perspective to see what can be inferred about the correct opinions and behaviours, which we should evidence as we follow our moral system.

IV

Proposals on the Individual

20

Biological Sex

"Biological sex should not determine what we are capable of, what we aspire to, or what we do in our life."

Anne-Marie Slaughter

Biological sex is defined so far as our Purpose as the genotypic differentiation of humans by those who have X chromosomes only who in common usage are called girls, women, or females, and those who have X and Y chromosomes who are termed boys, men, or males. These terms are used interchangeably in this work and can be understood to refer to the genotypic sex as defined here. Both of these genotypic groups are necessary to the continuation of human life, requiring the union of both genotypic classes gametes to reproduce. In our species' case, the female alone has the distinction of fulfilling the arduous role of gestating the young.

This gestational function forms the primary distinction between the human sexes. It is this distinction that forms the only proper division between men and women. This conclusion is not to deny the general phenotypic differences between males and females or imply that women are simply men with wombs. Indeed, each of us needs only to look around ourselves or consult with our experience to determine that, in the aggregate, women and men differ significantly from each other. These aggregated differences hold true in all areas from mental processes to physical abilities to each group's propensity to suffer from certain diseases. However, these differences, while real, when taken as averages, they are not absolutes except in so far as they causally relate to the gestational function.

Take, for example, the general fact that women are physically smaller than men. This is indeed true; in any given population, more women will be smaller than the statistical mean for that society than men. However, this does not mean that any given woman will be smaller than any given man. The same follows for other average characteristics of women compared to men: the supposed greater people focus, higher nurture instinct, lower aggression levels, or any of the other stereotypical female traits or their converse masculine trait. While, in general, it is true that a man may be more aggressive than a woman, it is not always so. One man may be more aggressive than any given women or vice versa just as any one person may be more aggressive than any other person.

If these traits are not consistent between the sexes, then it logically follows that they must not be essential elements of the thing itself. Based on this definition, it is a logical necessity that men and women are defined by their genotype (XX or XY), not their particular behavioural traits. This definition holds true even if phenotypically they present with atypical sexual characteristics, are reproductively unsound, or suffer from genetic abnormalities such as Klinefelter Syndrome (XXY), Superman Syndrome (XYY), or Turner Syndrome (X) to list just a few. If a person has a Y chromosome, they are male, and they are a female if they do not.

Having established the distinction in our species between the two genotypes of male and female, we must now discuss the roles of each and any differences in treatment that are appropriate due to the distinction of sex. This discussion is necessary due to the focus on reproduction as a key requirement for the achievement of the primary path of the Individual Purpose. This focus, coupled with women's unique gestational abilities, it is natural to wonder if the role of women and men in a community influenced by this philosophical position may differ from that in the current individual-focused society.

Some individuals have wondered if the renewed focus on family and children must come at the expense of women's gains in the world of work since the 1960s and 1970s. If women and girls are encouraged to have children again, they wonder 'if this is a dog whistle to those who would place women back in domestic servitude'. This regressive reaction could not be further from the truth; however, it does warrant a clear explanation to avoid misunderstanding. As such, the next chapter will discuss discrimination, starting with discrimination based on sex.

21

Discrimination

"Equality is not the empirical claim that all groups of humans are interchangeable; it is the moral principle that individuals should not be judged or constrained by the average properties of their group."

Steven Pinker, The Blank Slate: The Modern Denial of Human Nature

Sex

Firstly, it is vital to reiterate that a woman is distinguished from a man only by the essential difference of their genotype consisting of only the X chromosome, which leads in a reproductively capable female to the ability to gestate children inside specialised organs unique to females. The possession or lack of these organs contributes to an individual's value only so far as the reproductive potential is accounted for in prioritisation. Namely only that those individuals (male or female) who are not reproductively fit have a lower priority due to their lower potential than other similar individuals. This conclusion means that women have not got a higher or lower priority than men or vice versa. This being the case, it must follow that women must have the same rights and responsibilities as men ameliorated only in relation to individual differences in capability (which are not primarily sex-related).

Women should, as a logical necessity of their equality of individual value, be able to do any task, fill any role, and hold any position that their personal and individual abilities suit them for. This equality of value between the sexes means that standards, qualifications, and requirements for any role should be uniform and based on the nature of the essential nature of the task or tasks commonly carried out. Just as it is logical for a person of either sex to be required to pass a legal knowledge examination before working as a lawyer, so should a person of either sex be required to pass a physical fitness examination tailored to the requirements of the job before they can be hired as a labourer. Or a prospective florist be required to demonstrate colour perception ability or other minimum requisites of that trade.

The fact that, in the aggregate, some roles may end up with more women than men or vice versa, is not an indication of the existence of an artificial inequality any more than the observation that boilermakers tend to be larger and more muscular than the average person or that salespeople tend to be more engaging than the average. Provided that the entry requirements are truly based only on the candidate's relevant personal qualities, the differentials will tend to be due to the natural injustice of nature. This natural injustice is the same injustice that dooms some to dullness and others to genius, more people to plainness and less to beauty, some to exceptional size and others to shortness. We cannot change this natural injustice, as such, we should seek after our own unique advantages no matter the cards we are dealt. Any discrimination not based on the essential nature of the role should be considered an evil that harms our communities, families, and selves and should be extirpated from our laws, culture, and selves. In the same way as sex differences are specious grounds for discrimination, so too is discrimination based on other non-relevant traits such as race, ancestry, or class.

Race

Race has no place in our thinking; it does not exist as it is popularly conceived and serves merely to distract from what is truly important. Race or an individual's phenotypic traits are irrelevant and misleading markers of an individual's character traits. While we as humans are quite naturally drawn to those who we perceive as being like us, an individual's complexion, eye colour, nose shape, etc. are poor indicators of similarity or difference. If one doubts this, one needs only to look around their friendship group at the differences between those who would be considered to be of the same race. How many of those, who are supposedly White, Black, Asian or Hispanic, have the same skin tone? What about hair colour, hair type, eye colour? When we start seriously looking at the multitude of differences between each of us, we quickly see the absurdity of what we call race.

To quote Martin Luther King, a 'person should be judged on the content of their character, not on the colour of their skin'. Skin colour or any other phenotypic feature of an individual is not an indicator of character or an individual's relation to you in the community. As such, we should ignore it, always asking only what relation the individual has to you and your Individual Purpose's achievement. If they are a citizen or not, if they will reciprocate the help you give to them or not. These are the variables that matter as such race should be consigned to the dustbin of history where it belongs.

Of course, this is not to ignore the real discrepancies in education, health, history, and life outcomes which plague many groups previously identified with particular races in our societies. Simply not recognising race anymore will no more by itself rectify these disadvantages than any other symbolic act such as apologies or constitutional recognition will. However, what it will do is end the self-reinforcing and erroneous distinction that people can be differentiated by the colour of their skin or other phenotypic features—allowing for the differentiating individuals by their abilities and character.

All the well-meant race-focused programs that have been implemented in the western world to alleviate disadvantage (if they have merit) could just as easily achieve their outcomes if they were focused on the individual citizens who are actually disadvantaged instead of the innately heterogeneous groupings that raced-based differentiation yields. After all, if you reject the hypothesis that an individual's racial/phenotypic attributes significantly affect their abilities, then what argument can be advanced to justify dividing people by these traits?

Surely, a child who struggles with math will need similar help if they have brown eyes, blue eyes, or any other eye colour. Similarly, surely an adult who struggles to read will benefit from reading programs irrespective of their hair colour. The same implicitly follows for all other disadvantages or challenges faced by those in our society. The core variable which dictates the efficacy of any help needed is never their phenotype, except where artificial constraints are imposed. Instead, the help required is influenced primarily by non-phenotypic attributes such as culture, attitude, and individual character. Therefore, by these variables and by need, we should focus our efforts and resources so that we can more effectively help those who need it.

Similarly, as in our discussion of sex, it follows logically that a person's phenotype does not impact their individual value. As such, they should be free to peruse any or all roles, positions, or occupations which they are individually suited to, being determined only based on the essential requirement of the role. Failing to do this, we will harm our communities, families, and selves, needlessly limiting our collective opportunities and reducing our collective welfare. If we are the discriminator, we will lose through the ill will engendered by the harm caused by phenotypic discrimination, the loss of productive benefits which will be forgone by favouring a less suitable candidate due to similar phenotype over a better one with a dissimilar phenotype. If we are discriminated against, we lose through the loss of opportunity and the direct detriment to achieving our Individual Purpose from poverty, loss of self-worth, and hopelessness. Either way, if we allow non-relevant considerations to colour our judgements, we lose no matter which side of the divide we are on.

Ancestry

As with race, ancestry has no place in the estimation of a person's value, rights, or character. We hold that a person's worth is demonstrated through consistent action and is not in any way dependant on lineage. While parents are responsible for the education and socialisation of their children, and as such should be judged in part by the actions of their children; being that it is assumed that they have, through the exertion of influence in the child's formative years, played a role in shaping the child, the child is quite distinct from the parents once they have achieved their majority. The child should gain no claim to rights above that of other citizens on behalf of their parent's or ancestor's actions, nor should they be deprived of rights less than that of other citizens based on their parent's or ancestor's actions.

This position is, in effect, a rejection of the pre-enlightenment ideas of the importance and value of birth. I.e., a rejection that a person's value is in any way associated with their birth. Just as we reject segregation or differentiation of individuals by their sex or phenotypic traits, we also categorically reject individuals' segregation or differentiation by their ancestry. Once a person has reached maturity, who their father or mother is or who they may have been related to is of no importance. Where your ancestors lived and how long they lived there for is again irrelevant. What god or gods they worshipped, what language they spoke, what education they had, what titles or deeds, good or bad, they did are again irrelevant to the valuation of the individual. The only differentiation between individuals should be based on the individual's own actions. I.e. If they earnt their citizenship, if they are good parents, spouses, citizens, etc. We discriminate between individuals on these factors as they are the factors that matter. They are the elements of a person that tell us of their character. They inform us if the person can be trusted to help us to fulfil our Individual Purpose, just as they can tell them if we can be trusted to do the same. These are all the things which ancestry, race, class, and all other non-character-based differentiation cannot tell us.

Class

Class like sex, race, and ancestry should not be considered relevant to the differentiation between individuals. Class, as it is meant here is, as defined by the Cambridge Dictionary, 'A group of people within society who have the same economic and social position'. In the western world, class is less important than it once was yet its influence is still apparent in the attitudes which those of different professions or socioeconomic situations consider each other. Those in prestigious professions may look down on those in less prestigious professions as being less valuable than they. Those with university educations may think they are smarter than those without. We, humans, are exceptionally creative in inventing stories to make ourselves feel superior. We claim superiority over the nations near us (especially if they are similar), see Scotland and England, Australia and New Zealand, Canada and the USA. Between the administrative divisions in our countries, see the North-South divide in England or the US or the East-West divide in Australia or Canada. We even find ways to divide ourselves inside our cities, suburbs, or even streets. The truth is, while they or we may do some things better or worse or we may prefer to live here or there or do one job or the other, the individuals whom you disparage are not that different from you.

The cleaner may be more intelligent than the CEO. The Canadian may spurn the stereotype and be a rude jerk while the stereo-typically brash American may be a retiring type. The person from the bad part of town may be more civilised and cultured than the person from the more exclusive suburb. None of us can know, so instead of falling prey to these divisions that rely on prejudice rather than fact, let us instead seek to withhold judgement of others until they provide us with grounds to judge.

Class distinctions should then be like race and sexual discrim-ination be forgotten. As with other non-relevant classes of division, we should studiously ignore the distinctions of class or profession and instead judge a person by their ability and character alone.

The Childless/Infertile

As the primary Purpose of life is held to be achieved through reproduction, it is crucial that we devote some time to discussing those individuals who do not have children either by choice, through infertility, or due to the effects of misfortune. It is worth reiterating that the Individual Purpose is achieved in three ways. Through successful reproduction, secondly, through your siblings' successful reproduction, and thirdly, if all else fails, through the survival of the species. If an individual does or cannot for whatever reason have children of their own, they can still achieve their Individual Purpose through the other two paths.

Their inability or choice to not reproduce does not excuse them from the duties of family or community and nor should it be seen as a ground for censure. Those of us who are fortunate enough to have children know the joy they bring. Imagine being denied this joy for whatever reason. While it is, of course, laudable to share the joy, which is found in the achievement of the individual Purpose to reduce the mistaken decision to abstain from the primary path voluntarily. Those individuals who cannot or will not, should not be discriminated against, and as in all other cases, they should be judged on their actions and characters alone. If they lose out on joy or their line fails, they and their families suffer, not you and yours. As such, with all other differences that are not relevant to assessing a person's character, withhold your judgment.

Sexual Orientation

No discussion of discrimination would be complete without a discussion of same-sex attracted individuals. By 'same-sex attracted individuals', we mean those individuals who feel a strong and persistent attraction to those of their biological sex, either exclusively or primarily. If, as is commonly held, this same-sex attraction is involuntary and unchangeable, then viewed from the perspective of the Purpose of life, these individuals must be considered as akin to the infertile and not suffer any discrimination due to their sexual orientation. As with all other people, the same-sex attracted should be judged based upon their individual abilities, actions, and character.

Character and Actions

Character and the actions by which it is revealed is the sole measure other than task-specific competence by which it is appropriate to discriminate between individuals. By character, we mean the moral or ethical qualities that a person holds and consistently manifests. By this, I do not mean to advocate discrimination as often practised by religions between adherents or non-adherents. But, instead, to suggest that if we aim to promote the survival and welfare of our families and communities, then it is a logical necessity that we reward and hold to those who act in ways which we judge as being beneficial to this aim and censure and avoid those whose actions we judge as harmful. This truth is logically inescapable as if we remember the framework for moral decision-making; we are barred from making decisions that harm our families or communities and compelled to act in ways that promote the welfare of the same.

If we can choose a new friend, employee, citizen, etc., which person is more likely to harm us our families or our communities? An individual who is careful with the truth, demonstrates care for those around them, and carries out their duties to their families and communities. Or an individual who lies regularly and is inconsistent with fulfilling their duties to their family or community, putting their enjoyment first. It is evident that the honest and reliable individual holds less risk here than the dishonest and unreliable one. Consequentially, the logic is inescapable that the individual with these positive character traits is the better choice, in the same way as the person with greater ability in a core element of the proffered role is a better choice than that of a person with lesser ability.

Considering the above and the conclusions of the previous sections, it is evident that as we aim to bring our actions into accordance with that which will promote the individual Purpose, as a general rule, we will seek to judge others only by the attributes that are relevant to their reliability or ability in assisting us to achieve the individual Purpose. On investigation, we find that these attributes are limited to ability and character. Traits have nothing to do with the common biases utilised in the past to divide and discriminate between people such as sex, race, ancestry, class and profession, sexual orientation, or if a person is fertile or not.

The two discriminable factors that we recognise, being "Ability" and "Character", require a more thorough treatment to remove any grounds for misunderstanding. Therefore, in the next chapters, we will discuss both of these and their respective elements in greater detail. We will begin with the simpler of the two—ability.

22

Ability

"Believe in yourself! Have faith in your abilities! Without a humble but reasonable confidence in your own powers, you cannot be successful or happy."
Norman Vincent Peale

Ability is to be understood narrowly as the minimum physical or emotional capacity possessed by an individual. This definition focuses on a person's innate ability, not their willingness or constancy in putting it into practice (which is dealt with in character). When we talk about ability concerning legitimate discrimination, we are talking about ability in the specific sense, not the general. By this, we mean that it must be limited to the ability or capacity that is inherently essential to the task contemplated for the ability to be a relevant factor in judging a person. These inherent capacities can be but are not limited to knowledge, strength, speed, endurance, courage, leadership, or belief (in religious roles).

For instance, the essential ability or attribute inherent to a manual labourer's role is naturally different from that of a medical doctor. A medical doctor requires a knowledge of the practical application of medicine. In contrast, a labourer requires physical strength and endurance sufficient to the exertions needed for the common tasks required of them. As these two requirements are inherent to the two roles, it is logical that those who would practice each occupation must possess the requisite ability to the level needed to carry out the desired function.

This statement is not to suggest that the individual who works as a doctor could not work as a labourer or the individual who works as a labourer could not work as a doctor. Quite the contrary, it is the position of this work that all people are conceived with similar inherent intellectual capacities. It is through experience, influence, and inclination that the apparent differences in their capabilities appear. Therefore, what makes a person dull is not a lack of capacity but rather a lack of exercise of the intellectual faculty. In this way, a labourer could, with sufficient intellectual effort, develop and acquire the ability to work as a doctor, in the same way as a doctor could, with sufficient physical exertion, do the job of a labourer.

Similarly, as the ability essential to the task is appropriate to discriminate for, those which are not critical to the task or, are to a greater extent than required for the task, are not appropriate to discriminate against. For instance, while the ability to be able to lift heavy weights is essential in the role of a weightlifter, it is not as essential in that of a shopkeeper. Therefore, while seeking to select a weightlifter for a competitive team, the individuals' required ability to lift will be exponentially greater than that required of a shop assistant who will be asked to lift boxes weighing less than 20kg. To expect the shop assistant to be able to lift more than that, which is genuinely essential for the role, would be inappropriate discrimination.

It is important to note here that an individual's physical abilities are heavily impacted by genetics. A small, petite individual will have to exert greater effort on physical tasks than a larger individual. Conversely, a smaller individual may find working in constrained spaces more pleasant than that of a larger person. Be this as it may, these natural injustices are not sufficient to allow for legitimate discrimination based on physical size or shape except for where the task has the essential characteristic of physical constraint. Such as that of cockpit size in fighter jets or certain maintenance tasks requiring a person to work in particularly constricted spaces. Therefore, while it is legitimate to require a person to demonstrate their ability to be able to do the required task, it is not legitimate to decide that a person is incapable only because it would be more challenging for them than for others based on appearances alone.

An example of this could be the case of a petite young woman who applies for a mechanical apprenticeship. To the experienced mechanic who conducts the interview, her physical appearance may indicate that she might struggle with the more physically demanding aspect of the trade due to her slight frame. This judgement may be correct, just as the converse judgement that a relatively larger man or woman who may find these aspects of the role more manageable. However, until the bias is tested, it cannot be relied on. Additionally, the other essential elements of the role must also be considered.

The mechanical trades require both minimum levels of strength due to the work's physical elements and the developed mental abilities of spatial reasoning and problem-solving. Therefore, to reject the young girl only based on her appearance would amount to unjust discrimination, which, due to its harmful effect on our communities and families, is disallowed by our ethical system. Therefore, to judge if the girl in our example has the requisite abilities for the apprenticeship, it is necessary to test in an impartial way her (and all other applicants) current abilities against the role's inherent requirements. Why this is so important is that we should aim to select the best person for the role from the applicants.

Suppose we instead choose to allow irrelevant considerations to influence us. In that case, we harm our families and communities through the effective theft of opportunity from the candidate and the theft from ourselves of the additional production that the best candidate will bring to the task. This focus on excellence will be discussed in more detail in the chapter on work, but for now, let's move on to the second of the legitimate grounds for discrimination—character.

23

Character

"Human greatness does not lie in wealth or power, but in character and goodness. People are just people, and all people have faults and shortcomings, but all of us are born with a basic goodness."
Anne Frank

As touched on previously, by character, we mean the moral or ethical qualities which a person holds and consistently manifests. Therefore, when we talk of character, we inevitably talk of good character modifying the word only in the negative when we talk of bad or a lack of character. We mentioned specifically in that section qualities such as honesty and adherence to duty. However, it is not always easy, to be honest, or to do what your duty compels you to. The proof of this is abundant around us. From us pitifully vowing the same resolutions year after year to leaders in politics or religion being caught doing the very acts that they condemn in others. As our Code requires of us steadfast adherence to our duties to our families and communities, and as the Purpose of these duties is nothing other than our families' survival, we cannot afford to simply shrug and say, 'next time' when we are faced with a hard choice. Therefore, it is vital that we understand the building blocks of good character and methods by which we can practice and refine ourselves so that we may face any crisis that confronts us with confidence and equanimity.

24

Wisdom

Wisdom is an essential part of character being as Aristotle said in his ethics, "The ability to deliberate well about which courses of action would be good and expedient". Wisdom is not a natural skill, so do not despair if this is something you struggle with. For as Seneca said in his famous letters to Lucilius, 'No man becomes wise by chance, but only through hard work'. Therefore, do not delay, seek after it immediately. Do not allow yourself to put off for another day the work which must be done today.

Wisdom is not knowledge, so to speak, but applied judgement (which requires knowledge and experience). As such, it cannot be taught, only discovered. Never possessed in its totality and only truly perceived in someone by others. By this, I mean that as wisdom is the exercise of judgement informed by experience and knowledge, it can, by its essential nature, only be developed in a person by their own efforts.

Wisdom cannot be taught but must be found. While a teacher

can help point the student on to the correct path, it is the student who must internalise the maximums. It is they who must integrate the truths into their behaviours and they who must judge rightly the time, place, and way to act to the right person to achieve the desired outcome.

Wisdom can never be possessed entirely as it is infinite. A person accounted as wise may be able to act with wisdom in a multitude of situations. However, as we are inherently finite and the possible variations of existence infinite, there is always a possibility that the individual, however wise, will misjudge the time, place, or way in which they should act and, consequently, act unwisely. Therefore, it can never be possessed completely.

Finally, wisdom can only truly be observed in others, not in oneself. This is because as wisdom is thought and reason is action, it can only be judged by its outcomes. You may mean well, but if the effect of your actions is disastrous, it cannot be wise. If wisdom is always to be sought but never fully possessed, how could anyone genuinely think themselves wise? If one did, they would either be fooling themselves or have imagined that they possess the unpossessable.

Therefore, if you seek the best way to achieve your Individual Purpose, seek first after wisdom. Seek to learn first how to judge situations and people rightly. Understand what is relevant to your judgement (their character and ability) and what is irrelevant (race, sex, etc.). Seek knowledge of the world, read the accounts of the greats, and seek after examples worthy of emulation. Look deeply into everything that appears before you.

Seek to understand if things are as they appear or (as is often the case) not. Seek in every case to use your own judgement, and most importantly, learn from the mistakes of both yourself and others. For as Otto von Bismarck is credited with saying, "Only a fool learns from his own mistakes. The wise man learns from the mistakes of others".

25

The Virtues

The virtues (meaning merit, valour or moral perfections) are in essence what good character is made of. These timeless qualities have been talked of for millennium. Coming to historical notice in the west through the works of Plato and Aristotle. These virtues have been endlessly repeated with the stresses placed on each one varies depending on the proponents' Purpose. Be they in the form of the chivalric codes, the seven virtues and deadly sins or right here. For us, as our worldview is much more similar to that of the ancients than to the pre-modern Christian mind, we will be best served by the original (agnostic) virtues. We will discuss each virtue in order of their importance and discuss how you may implement them in your life.

Honour

Honour is a word not used much these days though it was the unwritten basis for civilisation itself throughout much of human history. The word honour means 'the quality of knowing and doing what is morally right' and 'to hold in great esteem'. For what we aim for in describing the good character necessary for the achievement of the Individual Purpose, nothing could be so apt.

Before we can start acting rightly, we must first know what act is right and what is wrong, and before we will act rightly, we have to want to. We must believe that in acting in the 'right' way, we will benefit ourselves somehow. This selfish requirement is doubly so when the act in question is difficult or unpleasant. Consider how the world's major religions explicitly offer this exchange to their devotees. Follow the injunctions of the faith and do what you are told is right, and in return, you will receive eternal life, escape from suffering, reincarnation higher up the hierarchy of life, etc.

It is an inescapable fact of existence that we only act when we see a benefit to ourselves. This being as it is, use it to your advantage. Seek through personal contemplation and the study of wisdom to understand and internalise the importance of your Purpose. Seek to understand how, by living in harmony with your life's Purpose, you will find that elusive good known as 'happiness'. Then hold the Purpose up as your aim and seek to build your personal honour around this aim.

Determine for yourself what actions in your life are helpful and what are harmful and work on consistently meeting the standards you aim for. Cultivate in your own mind an image of the person you want to be and hold yourself to account when you fail. Honour is, in essence, a personal conception of dignity, though the implied judgement of others much strengthens it.

Therefore, once you have deliberated on the standards you wish to judge and be judged by, do not keep them to yourself. Tell others so that they can hold you to account. This is essential as we often find that it is easier to maintain our intentions when there is external accountability. Who among us has not told themselves, "I'll start exercising tomorrow" or "I'll quit 'X' next month" or I'll keep to that 'diet' next time, etc.? We fail in these well-meaning assertions because, when it is just us, we always have an out. 'No one knows', we reason; therefore, we can break our word to ourselves without consequence. This weakness is true of all of us so, therefore, do not give yourself an out, tell someone.

Charles de Gaulle, the leader of the Free French and Post-war president of France, was by all account a very self-disciplined man, yet he seems to have known this secret. De Gaulle was like many people in the 1940s, a heavy smoker. In 1944, he decided to quit. As anyone who has tried to quit smoking will attest, this is not easy to achieve. De Gaulle announced his determination to the word and quit. When asked about it later, he said, 'It was very hard to quit and I would have smoked again except I was unwilling to be seen to break my word'. If a man such as he can benefit from the accountability of strangers, then so can we.

Therefore, of all the virtues, honour is the most important. With wisdom, it is the base on which everything else is built. And the package in which all the other virtues are contained. To have honour is to know and do what is right to achieve the Purpose which we hold to be good. To accomplish this and be accounted as honourable, we need the other virtues as well. Our aim should be to be able to truly and without qualification judge ourselves as honourable. To do this, we need the courage to start down the road to virtue.

Courage

Courage is the second of the virtues that we will discuss. Courage in the sense we use it here means more than simply the ability to do something frightening. It is to be understood as Aristotle describes it in his ethics. 'The virtue of action in the face of danger that is guided by wisdom being proportionate to the situation sitting between recklessness and cowardice". This definition means that courage means to act even when there is danger in a way that harmonises with the Purpose. Courage is necessary as we would be incapable of making any decisions or making any move where there was resistance without it.

Courage is not always about facing death; it can be about taking on a new challenge, changing jobs, deciding to change a harmful habit, or even believing something unpopular or controversial. Like all the virtues, Courage requires practice as Aristotle succinctly puts it, 'A man becomes what his habits are. If he never stands his ground, he becomes a coward, if he never gives way, he becomes rash'. Therefore, seek to use your judgment and stand for what is necessary to achieve your Individual Purpose, i.e., that which promotes your family and community's long-term welfare. Equally, though, refrain from actions that you cannot prevail in and which would only harm your family and community's welfare.

In this sense, courage is synonymous with prudence. Picking only those fights that you can win and biding your time where you cannot prevail. Or as Sun Tzu said in the Art of War, "Who wishes to fight must first count the cost". Our aims are not figurative or speculative; they are concrete. We aim for the good of our families and communities. This aim means that, at times, we will be forced to choose the least bad outcome for our families and communities. Sometimes acting courageously will require warlike actions and aggression. Yet other times, it will require humility, and for us to act in a way that others may judge as cowardly.

Take Adlai Stevenson's example in the film 'Thirteen Days', when the US cabinet is discussing an invasion or blockade of Cuba as the only two options: "There, uh, there is a third option. With either course we undertake the risk of nuclear war, so it seems to me that maybe one of us in this room should be a coward... so, I guess I'll be it. A third course is to strike a deal". This courageous action was what the situation required, and while presented in a film, it mirrors Adlai's actions in real life. Adlai was considered a coward by many after the crisis though as he said, "I know that most of those fellows will consider me a coward for the rest of my life for what I said today, but perhaps we need a coward in the room when we are talking about nuclear war".

Courage, as touched on before, is required in the small crises of life as much as in the big. It is a virtue built on consistent and conscious action. It is the second of the virtues as it is required to allow us to change. We must develop the courage to utilise our wisdom to determine right from wrong and to set the Purpose that we have discovered as the basis for our personal honour. It requires courage to change or do things differently from those around you; it is not easy to walk against the crowd. If you find that the truth is different from what you had believed it to be, you need the courage to follow that truth to where it leads. It may require you to renounce your faith in what your family believes. It may lead you to act in ways that others see as wrong or just misguided. In each case, courage is essential. To practice your courage, force yourself to do what you believe to be right, to speak (with wisdom) the truth and focus your actions on your family and community's welfare. Be safe but do not allow fear to control you.

However, as with honour and wisdom, courage is not enough alone in building a worthy character. If we are to live a life that will promote our families' and communities' welfare, then we also need to develop the virtue of truthfulness or honesty.

Honesty

Honesty is the attribute of speaking and acting honestly, i.e. acting in a non-deceptive way and speaking in such a way as the truth can readily be discerned from it. Aristotle defines honesty or truthfulness in a way that aligns substantively with that of our aims. In his ethics, Aristotle defines honesty as a 'mean state between that of the exaggeration of the bragger and the devaluation or false modesty of the reserved'. I.e. honesty is the claiming of what is one's own and not what is someone else's. An example of this is the common occurrence at work where your success in a particular project or crisis is due in part to the idea or help of another. Being honest is claiming the rightful recognition of your efforts while ensuring that the one who helped you is acknowledged as well. By contrast, honesty is not claiming all the credit or claiming no credit; it is only claiming the credit due to us as judged by an impartial observer.

For many of us, this is hard to do. Especially if you have been raised in a British influenced society such as the UK, Australia, New Zealand, or Canada, you will likely have been raised to show modesty and downplay your achievements. This modesty is well and good, but there is a difference between being modest and refusal to accept praise stereotypical of the English upper class.

To be honest, therefore, is to seek to judge yourself and others impartially. Taking care to act and speak truthfully. We have covered why lying, stealing, and deceit are harmful in the chapter on morality. As such, we will not go over the same ground here except to reiterate that lying, deceit, and theft harm our families and communities by increasing the costs and risks in every act and exchange.

Some may counter that little so-called white lies are far from being harmful and serve a positive social function. They say that when we lie and say that we are busy when we'd rather stay in alone, we spare the feelings of the one we lie to. When we lie at work and say we have done the task and then rush off to do it, we are protecting ourselves. To these objections, I say that they are misguided. Far from being harmless, these little lies are the foundation for dissolution.

Now, I am not saying that we should act boorishly and without consideration for the situation or of others' feelings, only that we should be truthful while exercising wisdom. Consider our two examples. What do you really gain by lying to your friend? If you really don't want to go out this one time, will they really not understand that you just want some time alone? And if the real reason is that you just don't want to go out with them, will they be any less perturbed if you put them off endlessly compared to if you just tactfully told them you have different interests? The lie, while the easier option, will not benefit you much if it is not discovered, but it will destroy your credibility if it is discovered.

With the example of the undone task, the lie is even more harmful than with the lie to a friend. By lying, you first harm yourself. You give yourself an excuse to not do the task or not to do the task as well or as promptly as you could. You allow yourself to do a worse job than you could and you attempt to hide your failure through deception. Consider if you forced yourself to be truthful. Would your boss really punish you for telling the truth and saying that you hadn't started it and would do it now? If they would, surely you are at fault for delaying when the consequences are so dire. Consider also what would happen if you were caught in the lie. If you found out your employee had lied to you about something so small, could you ever trust them again? Again, the risk is far greater than the transitory reward. Instead, preserve your honour and seek through your actions to demonstrate your integrity. Save that most valuable commodity for when it may be needed to protect your family and community. For as with everything generally wrong, there are exceptions.

As to ourselves, honesty is necessary to the development of character as it will force us if we practice it and incorporate it into our honour code to judge ourselves honestly. Where we are deficient and where we are superior both require the practice of truthfulness. We must utilise our hard-won wisdom to judge what is right and wrong, be courageous enough to pursue it, and be honest enough to recognise where we can improve and where we have failed. Do not give yourself an out. Keep track of your promises and keep them. If you fail, admit it, apologise, and do better next time. The next virtue we need to develop a character worthy of emulation is patience.

Patience

The Cambridge Dictionary defines patience as "The ability to wait, or to continue doing something despite difficulties, or to suffer without complaining or becoming annoyed". This virtue is the fourth of our virtues, and it is vital to the achievement of character. If you are a mortal like all of us, then you will fail at some time. You will make a mistake, misjudge the situation, or simply tire of the exertion of becoming better, of deliberating to identify the best action to promote the welfare of your family or community. Or you may simply, without thinking at all, go astray for a while. What is sure is that even if it is not you, it will be others. Patience is indispensable in catching yourself, your friend, or your loved ones having gone astray and turning back to the correct path. It is indispensable in simply restraining yourself when you are confronted with those who still act without reason be they great or small. Whether it is the individual driving too fast in the parking lot or the person who will not let you merge on the freeway. Your boss making a decision which seems close to madness or the government of the day acting disgracefully. Or perhaps it was you getting drunk, gambling, or doing any of the things you have decided to be harmful. In each case, patience is needed either with yourself, others, or with the vicissitudes of fortune.

The patience to restrain the frustration of the moment and seek after the reason. The patience to get up the next day and try again. The patience to persevere with what you know to be right even when everyone gives up. You can have wisdom, honour, courage, and honesty for a time, but without patience, you will not possess them in the long-term. Life is a procession of chance events—some good and some bad. No matter how wise we are or how carefully we lay our plans sometimes, things go poorly (for there is always the chance of disaster). Those in possession of real character will recognise this and wait patiently for the wheel of fortune to turn in their favour once more. Never despairing, but maintaining their honour and their hope.

To practice this virtue, remember 'vos can tatum control te', or you can only control you. This maxim, as held by the Stoics such as Roman Emperor Marcus Arillus and by the former slave, Epictetus, is meant to remind us that we only control our reactions to the world, not the world itself. In a real sense, we are only as unhappy as we choose to be. To build your patience and enhance your happiness, try biting back your frustration when that 'person' cuts you off when you are reversing, and instead of calling them a name, ask yourself a question such as "why are they in such a hurry?". If the car won't let you merge on the freeway, derail your anger by asking, "I wonder why they chose to do that?". Getting angry will not do you any good, you are not going to chase them down and punch them (and would be wrong to do so), so instead, ask yourself why that person did what they did. It may have been a mistake, they may have misjudged the situation, maybe they were distracted, or perhaps they were angry that someone had done the same thing to them. In any case, it is doubtful that you have not ever done as they have done.

By asking these questions, you will preserve your serenity and happiness, build your patience, and free yourself to live better, instead of being angry and perhaps inadvertently doing another wrong like that which angered you. You will be calm and can, therefore, set the example you want. You will be able to allow others to merge in traffic, be able to happily wait for people to back out of their parking spots and even to maintain a serine detachment when your boss does something you disagree with, or the government messes up.

The benefits you will see will grow as your patience improves.

You will be happier; you will be able to influence your children or partner, workmates, or bosses positively. If you doubt this, think back to your childhood, did you ever listen to your parents when they were angry? And, just as importantly, you will develop the strength needed to preserve in your pursuit. The next virtue we will discuss is temperance. This virtue, as with the rest, requires the virtues that go before if it is to be borne.

Temperance

Temperance or moderation in action is the fifth of our virtues. It is the fifth virtue as its exercise depends on the possession of both wisdom and the first four virtues honour, courage, honesty, and patience. While temperance is associated in the modern world with vices such as drinking, gambling, and the like, we use it in a broader sense. When we talk of temperance, we talk of the pursuit of pleasure or goods that are surplus to that which is required to achieve the Purpose. We are talking of vices such as drinking, the use of drugs, gambling, sex, the pursuit of wealth, of honour, or of power. Each of these things can, in certain situations, be positive as with wealth, honour, power, or sex where used for procreation or the mutual pleasure of partners. However, when used or pursued to excess or in a harmful way to your family or community, they are harmful and hateful to the individual and society.

The virtue of moderation is the exercise of wisdom in conjunction with the previous virtues to determine the proper limits that one should place on everything. The appropriate limits to each are different for everyone. Some people can drink socially, and some cannot. The limits for each differs in quantity but not the effect. Once the act begins to harm your family or community, it is time to reconsider it. The same holds for those things which are generally considered goods such as earning money or chasing success.

Unless you have been exceedingly fortunate, you will need to work. We generally work for economic reasons rather than for any love of the task. It's a necessary sacrifice, and to a point, it is an integral part of achieving the Purpose for at least one of the partners in any family. However, it is common for this necessary good to be taken beyond its bounds and to begin to harm the family and or the community. This exceeding of the proper bounds of a good is the case for workaholics who, mistaking the correct bonds for their labour, continue working past the point where they start to harm their families through their absence. They wrongly believe that the more money they earn, the better they are doing their role of providing for their family. Temperance here is to understand that economic work is a means to an end of providing for the long-term welfare of their families, not the end in itself. By working without absolute need past the point where it begins to harm their families, they are failing in their duties.

Remember that your duty to your family is not to provide them luxuries, but merely to ensure that they are protected from harm, clothed, fed, and supported emotionally. If while trying to give them more you work beyond what is proper, you achieve in providing for their material needs but fail in providing for their emotional needs. Your failing is in prioritising one thing to the exclusion of all else.

The same also applies to those who are driven by greed. The greedy make the mistake of thinking the path to provide for their families' welfare lies solely in the possession of wealth. In pursuing this good, they often harm others in their communities. Destroying all who stand in their way and disposing of their workers and colleagues when there is a profit to be made. In trying to benefit their families, they harm them by removing their best support, that of the community. In their misguided pursuit of profit above all, they lose sight of what is essential, and in the end, they suffer for it. This criticism is not to condemn entrepreneurial endeavour, quite the opposite. Wealth, be it the possession of it, or especially the creation of it for yourself and those in your community, is laudable. However, it is good only as with all other things to the point where it begins to harm yourself, your family, or your community. Temperance is the exercise of wisdom to know when enough is enough.

As with wealth, so it is with power. Power is a tool by which the aspirant wishes to set wrongs to right. Yet as has often been noted, 'power corrupts'. In this case, temperance is to set a guard on yourself and ask if the price of power is worth it. If the action will harm, is it essential to the Purpose or not? If it is not essential, then decline the honour or the power. Wisdom is to prefer right over power and the good of your family to that of worldly glory. If you doubt this, then consider how few of those accounted great can claim the success which the humblest family man can, that of the continuation of his family or their happiness. Napoleon had but one child who did not survive to adulthood, Julius Caesar died without issue (adopting his nephew, Octavian). Winston Churchill had many children who lived and died unhappily. The same unhappy tale seems to be the lot of the families of those who the world accounts as great, be they kings or prime ministers.

Surely, we who aim for our families' good would do well to carefully consider the costs of power and exercise restraint to avoid the harm to our families, which so often is the corollary of power.

Therefore, if you would achieve your Individual Purpose, culti-vate temperance in all your actions. If you would drink, drink but not to the point of harm and stop if you can't. When you work, seek to keep sight of the reasons you work and the costs you bear. We would be wise to be cautious of power and if we are called to it, to seek carefully to do what is right and to place it down as soon as we are able to do so. In essence, we would seek to have just enough to fulfil our duties, being happy if more comes to us yet not chasing it. Being as content in private obscurity as in the halls of power and always placing the good first and always if we possess power seeking to be just.

Justice

Justice is the sixth of our virtues, and it is perhaps the most obscure of the virtues. Of course, we have all heard of 'justice', and perhaps we even think that we know what it is. It is generally thought of as a form of fairness or giving to each what they deserve, setting inequality to rights, etc. This definition is both correct and incorrect in our conception. Justice is indeed about fair, consistent, and impartial treatment, but it is not about acting fairly or for the involved parties' interest. It is instead about acting in the interest of the community.

This conclusion may seem paradoxical. Surely justice is the same no matter whom it concerns. But this is not true. What is just for one is often unjust for another. Consider the case of a bankrupt. It would likely be just to the creditor to ensure that their money is returned in full, however, providing that the debtor has not acted fraudulently, would it be just to them? The debtor would likely feel that they have suffered more and that it would be just to allow them a second chance and free them from the debt. It would seem that whichever way the judge decides, one of them will be treated unjustly. This outcome is the same, even if the justice is consistent and impartial.

What is missing is the consideration of the commonweal. Instead of asking what is just for the individual, we should instead ask what is best for the community as a whole. In this particular case, does the loss of an investment by an investor involve worse harm than the impact which harsh bankruptcy laws have? Without delving into the economics of the problem too deeply in general, it has been found that allowing more generous treatment to bankrupts not involving fraud would seem to offer greater benefits to the community compared to prioritising the investor. Justice is not limited to the legal sphere; indeed, it is a virtue as it is general in nature.

We should show justice in acting fairly, consistently, and

impartially in all things. We should exercise justice in the hiring and firing of employees, in the judging or playing of games, in the disciplining or rewarding of our children, and in the imposition of laws and rules. In each situation, we should determine what standard to enforce based on the achievement of the Individual Purpose and enforce it uniformly. This virtue is based on the reality that nepotism or the favourable treatment of people based on their prior relationship to you or other non-relevant traits while appearing to offer benefits is, in fact, a harmful imposition on your, your families', and the communities' welfare.

This is because of the random nature of reality and the in-evitable turning of the wheel of fortune as well as the inter-connectedness of our communities. For every benefit gained by nepotism to the one with power, harm is done to another in their community. Nepotism appears to benefit those who practice it as they and the other insiders form a tight group and share out the benefits. Over time, as this group becomes more insular and focused on maintaining and enhancing their privileges, and less on maintaining and achieving excellence, they go into decline and are eventually destroyed. The harmful effects of nepotism are as relevant in a small business as in a great state. When we are unjust, we plant the seeds of our own destruction.

Of course, as with all virtues, justice requires the exercise of wisdom and the virtues. It takes wisdom to determine what is just based on the community's needs, courage to make the just decision even if it costs you friends or position. The honesty to examine your motivations to keep them focused on the true

Purpose and not be distracted by illusionary gain. The patience and moderation to persevere and to know the right limits and to not exceed them. I.e. to punish enough to dissuade others but no more than is necessary or when harm must be done to know how to as little as or as much as needed but no more and finally to be magnanimous in power or success.

Magnanimity

Magnanimity is held to be different from generosity by Aristotle in that it is to do with great things while generosity is held to be to do with small. This is but a semantic difference which we will abandon. When we talk of magnanimity, we mean it to mean a generosity of spirit, especially in triumph. We hold it to be part of generosity as to be generous is synonymous with superiority of some form. Consider the act of charity, is it not termed generous to give precisely as those to whom charity is given are held to have less? The same is often said of a leader who credits their success solely to their team; they are termed generous with their praise. Magnanimity is, therefore, the virtue of being generous when in possession of good fortune.

This magnanimity of spirit is a virtue as it is natural when fortune is smiling on us to mistake her favour as being settled when it is but transitory. Or as Boethius laments in his Consolation of Philosophy, "Mad Fortune sweeps along in wanton pride, Uncertian as Euripus' surging tide; Now (she) tramples mighty kings beneath her feet; Now she sets the conquered in the victors seat. She heeds not the wail of hapless woe, But mocks the griefs which from her mischief flow. Such is her sport; so proveth she her power; And great the marvel, when in one brief hour, she shows her darling lifted high in bliss, then headlong plunged in misery's abyss." Magnanimity is primarily the wise remembrance of this age-old truth. Generously ignoring past insults and harms, and instead seeking after the Purpose with wisdom and virtue. Recognising that 'Sic transit gloria mundi' all glory is fleeting and that just as you are up in the moment, so they may be up when you are down.

This tendency does not apply just to those who experience great fortune. It applies equally to each one of us. If you see a person who is struggling, help them up without the expectation of reward. Imagine it was you who was down and act accordingly. This obligation is as valid if the person's misfortune is their own fault or not. Each one of us is where we are due at least in part through the agency of chance. One different roll of the dice and we may have ended up as the homeless or the addicted. Don't risk your welfare or that of your family, but within your ability's limits, help where you can and be generous to others. Especially, as you judge them, remember it is easy to blame but hard to get up once you have fallen.

Friendliness

The eighth and final virtue that we will discuss is that of friendliness or being a friend to others. This virtue should be understood as a willingness to initiate and act as a friend to those whom you come in contact with. What is meant by this is that we should treat everyone we meet as we would a person we were or at least wanted to be friends with.

This virtue means that we should make the effort to be genuinely interested in them for no other purpose than as a person, or as Kant said in his foundations of ethics, 'Treat each person never ever merely as a means to an end, but always at the same time as an end in themselves'. Approach each person from the position that they might prove to be a friend for often people simply will consciously or unconsciously mirror how they are treated. If treated with respect and care, they will generally do the same.

The virtue of friendliness demands more than merely the reflection of others. It requires us to put ourselves out there and to utilise all the other virtues we have discussed to seek to be a friend to those around us. If you are naturally shy, be courageous. If you are reluctant to do so, be honest. Why? Is it because of the legitimate reasons for discrimination or is it simply because of some less noble reason? Be patient and moderate in your judgements; not everyone is like you, and not everyone will prove to be a friend but be just and give them a chance. If they prove to be unworthy of your friendship by acting in a hurtful or harmful way, be magnanimous and move on, don't hold their ignorance or foolishness against them. If you judge it as wise, give them another chance. If not, just let them be. The virtue is in the honest attempt. But I assure you, more often than not, the person you might have hesitated to approach will turn out to be worth the effort. For as Galileo is supposed to have remarked: "I have never met a man so ignorant that I couldn't learn something from him".

Friendliness is, in essence, the willingness to be a friend to others. To teach what you know if requested, to help where you can, but more than anything, simply be open to others. It is not a suggestion to let strangers into your home or place yourself in dangerous situations but simply to be available. If you see a person in danger, be a friend and help them. If you see someone sad, then lend them an ear. If someone is struggling, help them. In short, be the friend or person that you would want to approach you if you found yourself in a similar situation.

With this, it is time to move from the issues which primarily are of the individual to the issues which pertain primarily to the community. Of course, there is much overlap between the two areas and what applies to the community also applies to the individual and vice versa.

V

Proposals on the Community

26

Political

"As soon as any man says of the affairs of the State "What does it matter to me?" the State may be given up for lost."
   Rousseau, The Social Contract

To determine the system most likely to support the community's Purpose in allowing the achievement of the Individual Purpose by its members, we must first briefly determine what general societal conditions are productive of this outcome and which are not.

It is logical to suppose that a society and the concurrent political system that will support the achievement of the individual Purpose will promote the actions and attitudes identified thus far as being positive contributors to the achievement of the Purpose. This means that while it is a given that a societal structure and political system that supports the members' survival and long-term welfare is essential, it is also preferable that it be structured to embrace the three elements of Community (Exclusivity, Affirmation, and Mutual Recognition). While simultaneously discouraging the negative forms of discrimination and encouraging the differentiation of individuals based on the qualitative elements of character, action, and individual capacity.

In theory, all forms of government and society from the tribal to the modern welfare state can fulfil these objectives. However, in practice, the nature of humanity is such that systems that lack strong restraints to the use and abuse of power are inevitably co-opted to benefit in groups to the wider community's detriment. This degradation of the common good has been the historical experience of humanity under systems and societal structures as diverse as feudalism, communism, fascism, and the plutocratic movements that rule in much of the developing world. In each case, the system that was initially created for the mutual benefit of the community members has been subverted to benefit a smaller sub-community. Therefore, it is logical that the society that is ideally structured to support the community's welfare will have traits that are resistant to the formation of faction and have strong limits and controls on the exercise of power.

Even if, hypothetically, society were composed of saints who always acted in accordance with the values expressed within this text, there would still be the need to restrain the exercise of power. The nature of the Purpose is that we are compelled to prioritise our friends' and families' welfare over that of others. This creates an impulse to exercise power in ways that may not always be in the wider community's interests. This impulse is natural to all humans and fundamentally laudable in its inspiration; however, it must be constrained through the establishment and enforcement of penalties that are sufficiently severe to impede and disincentivise those who possess the ability to exercise governmental power from unduly exercising it to their own benefit.

This level of constraint on the use and abuse of power is only likely to be possible in a democratic and egalitarian society that has high levels of transparency and citizen engagement. A general proposal of how such a society could be structured will be discussed in the next few chapters. The most crucial element in this societal structure is the community itself, and that is what we will discuss first.

Citizenship

Citizenship, or formal membership of a community as we mean it here, is to be understood as an individual title which carries a sense of belonging or commitment to a particular polity. While, like with all words, its meaning is arbitrary, it undeniably carries with it a sense of mutual responsibility between members. It is also a legal term in the western world, denoting the possession of rights and duties of the possessor towards and from the polity. It is a central proposition of this work that, as communities exist to promote the community members' survival and welfare, it is reasonable that mutual loyalty is required between them.

Citizenship should be realigned to support this mutual loyalty. Citizenship should be singular in that each individual who has citizenship of the community should renounce all other citizenships or incompatible group loyalties. The rationale for this is simple. If we are to hold that citizenship of a community is to require of us joint mutual protection and support, then we should wish to limit that support to those who we can be sure will support us in turn. How can we be sure of this support if an individual can pick and choose their loyalty depending on whichever benefits them most at the moment? By making citizenship singular and exclusive, we can increase the costs of disloyalty and better avoid split loyalties.

This conception of citizenship would, in addition to requiring the renunciation of all other national citizenship, by its nature, also require the renunciation of incompatible group memberships. By this, we mean civil, religious, or other groups that claim individual loyalty to the group in any way that is incompatible with the citizen's duties to the community. Some examples of these groups could be the seventh day Adventists Church or other religious orders that require pacifism from their members, Islam which calls for loyalty to the Ummah or Islamic community, revolutionary or separatist organisations which call for the destruction of the community, etc.

To further emphasise citizenship's essential nature as being one of communal responsibility, it is not enough to allow people to gain citizenship passively. Instead, it must be earnt through personal action and affirmation of both the duties and rights of citizenship. The best approach to this affirmation is to combine the acceptance of citizenship's responsibilities with a period of service to the community. During this service, an individual would mix with other citizens, forming bonds outside their local area, and through their labour, help to defend and support their fellow citizens.

How this could work in practice is that upon reaching legal majority, a child of a citizen or a resident could opt to affirm their citizenship. They would formally renounce all other citizenships and greater loyalties outside of the community and legally accept the responsibilities of the citizen. They would then complete a period of national or community service. This service would ideally be both civil and military, preparing and educating the citizen to perform their duties to the polity actively. Upon completing this service, the individual would receive their formal citizenship and be held to possess full civil and political rights. These rights should include the right to work in all professional fields, work in the civil service, hold political office, vote, serve in the military, act as a magistrate, possess weapons, and any other rights that seem proper to be restricted to citizens alone.

All those who choose not to affirm their citizenship would remain 'national residents', retaining the right for themselves and their children to remain in the nation permanently and having the right to own property, work in all non-restricted fields, and live wherever they please. National residents would occupy a secondary position in society due to their choice in not affirming and bearing the duties of citizenship.

This differentiation is based on character and action, and through the active process of socialisation inherent in com-

munal service such a societal structure, if properly implemented, would foster in the citizen a personal commitment
and engagement with 'the good' of the wider community.
This communal engagement is the essential foundation of all
the other structures that are needed to allow for a genuinely
democratic, egalitarian, and transparent society required to
ensure that governance in the interest of the community
persists in the long-term.

Governance

The form of governance that would seem to offer the best
chance for this outcome is democracy. This is due to the typically greater engagement and association with the government
of the average citizen compared to that of other systems. Of
course, there is a multitude of so-called democratic systems
extant. As such, we must begin our discussion on governance by
defining what we mean by democracy. Democracy, as discussed
here, means a 'system whereby all citizens exert direct power
and influence over the government of their community'.

The implementation of real democracy, as defined here, has
proven to be difficult historically. With a broad franchise (direct
democracy), it is difficult and burdensome for the electors to
gain sufficient reliable information to be across each issue
they are called to determine. This burden leads inexorably
to either poor quality decisions or low engagement, both of
which serve to discredit direct democracy. At the same time,
a democracy where the franchise is heavily limited tends to

become aristocratic or oligarchic due to the concentration of power. Various methods have been attempted to resolve these issues. These attempts range from the Swiss federation system to the British and Commonwealth Parliamentary systems and the American influenced Republican model popular in the Americas.

The problem with all these systems is that they either place on the citizen, as in the Swiss model, the requirement to judge on issues that they lack sufficient information to evaluate correctly, or they place the citizen in the position of selecting candidates to (at least nominally) represent them. The direct model is slow and burdensome to the citizen, requiring those who wish to judge matters well the investment significant of time and effort to gather the appropriate information (some of which may not be available to the general public). While, on the other hand, in representative democracies, the representatives have (at least theoretically) time and opportunity to investigate and inform themselves on the subject they are examining. While due to sweeping powers being vested with the parliament, they can move more swiftly when required.

While these two systems are sitting somewhat on the extreme ends of the democratic systems that exist, they suit our Purpose in demonstrating the flaws in both the direct and representative forms of democracy. What is then desirable is a form of demo-cratic governance which combines both the citizen engagement and involvement of the direct form with the speed and ability to fully inform those who must judge which is the strength of the representative form. To fully enunciate such a system would require more time and space than this current work would allow, so we will limit ourselves to the broadest of strokes.

A possible system that meets this need is to couple a parliament of elected representatives with a limited form of direct democracy. Under this hybridised system, the parliament would, as it currently does in British-influenced nations, retain its position as the primary chamber for the proposition and debate of legislation dealing with law, national policy, and financial administration. However, they would be denied the power to legislate or enact these acts on their own authority.

The figurative second chamber could consist of citizens chosen by lot from each electorate or district to review the proposed legislation and either pass or reject it. A simple method for selecting the citizens called to this function exists in the jury duty system where all citizens are placed in a pool for call-up, and once called, are removed from the pool for a set period of time. With modern technology, it would be possible to allow for councils of say one hundred to be called in each district or electorate to consider each piece of legislation passed by the parliament. Each of these councils, meeting either as a single group or in small local groupings in their respective districts, could then as a single national council hear presentations from members of the parliament who wish to speak in support or opposition to the proposed act before giving or withholding their consent.

This method would offer the benefits of both representative democracy and direct democracy. The parliament would retain its restraining power through control over what legislation is drafted and submitted to the citizen councils for assent. The average citizen would gain the power that has always been promised but never delivered in modern democracies—the power to rule themselves. Each citizen could expect to be called to consider (based on average parliamentary legalisation rates) one act every 3-5 years at both the national and state/provincial levels. As this draw would be random both in timing and in the members' composition, it would be highly likely to foster a greater sense of ownership and engagement with the governmental system and the nation as a whole amongst the citizens. As the citizens would hold the decision-making power by lot, they would possess the power to prevent the erosion of their liberties and prevent the abuse of power by any group.

A by-product of this citizen-determined government would be a realignment of the laws and legal system to better align with the citizens' expectations. This realignment would depend on the times and composition of the citizens, so we will not discuss it further here. However, due to the legal systems' opacity, there are some general reforms necessary to support the community's Purpose.

Legal

The legal systems in at least the English-speaking common law nations pay lip service to transparency and openness. However, if you take the time to look past the appearances, you will quickly discover that much of what presents as transparency and openness is merely a façade. The judiciary continues to be selected from the insiders of the legal profession. Their decisions are generally obscured (at least partly) from the public, and furthermore, they are secure from review and disapprobation by the separation of powers and contempt of court laws.

As with the discussions of governance in the previous chapters, there is insufficient space in this work to explore the benefits and disadvantages of the legal system in even a single country. As such, we will limit ourselves to several broad observations and general proposals that seem to offer the promise of benefiting those of us who seek to find the best path to achieving our Individual Purpose. First, it is logical to consider why the legal system exists or why it should exist.

The legal system exists as a method of judging offences against the community of which it belongs. If, as we have discussed, the community exists to support the achievement of the individual Purpose by the families and individuals which form it, and the government of a community exists to facilitate this communal welfare through administrative actions, it follows that the legal system exists or at least should exist to ensure that citizens of the community can resolve their disputes with each other in a fair, consistent, and impartial manner.

In essence, all legal disputes are between individuals, whether they be civil or criminal. In both criminal and civil cases, one party is accused of acting in a way contrary to the general standards held by a particular society. In both cases, the law should seek to provide in a consistent, transparent, and impartial manner a judgement that serves the interests of the community as a whole.

This method is different from seeking to provide justice that changes depending on the individual. Consider the case of murder. To do justice to the victim is impossible as no one can give them their life back. To do justice to the victim's family as is commonly called for would result in the perpetrator's death. However, invariably this justice as it is decried as unjust to those on the other side.

The perpetrator's defenders will often state that the offender made a mistake, acted without intent to kill, or could be rehabilitated. They point to those who have been spared and have changed. Furthermore, let's consider the offender's family. It is arguable that in providing justice to the family of the murdered, we necessarily do an injustice to the perpetrator's family. Denying a parent their child, a child, their father, or a lover.

Instead, if we focus on the welfare of the whole community, it is simplified. We only need to ask what sentence will be most likely to promote the interests of the community. Suppose it was beneficial that murderers be allowed to murder without repercussion. In that case, no penalty would need to be applied. If, however, murder is not advantageous to the social good (which it is not), then a penalty that on balance is likely to make murder less common should be applied.

Whatever the outcome, it is vital that the outcome be consistent, transparent, and fair, i.e. the penalty for any given crime of similar severity should be the same with no significant variation between judge, location, and defendant.

To ensure that this consistency is achieved, the courts must be transparent and accountable to the citizens. This statement does not suggest that the judges should be exposed to pressure to rule one way or the other on any specific case. Merely, that judges' decisions and sentences be available in the specific and aggregate to the public and that judges be exposed to periodic review and removal by the citizens in the areas they preside.

This transparency and general accountability would help ensure that judicial officers' decisions would become or at least be seen to be consistent with the expectations of the residents in their area, and through the comparability of judgements, help to ensure greater consistency in outcome throughout jurisdictions. We will finish our introductory discussion of the community by talking of work and its role in achieving the Purpose.

27

Work

"Our labour preserves us from three great evils —
weariness, vice, and want."
Voltaire (Candide)

Work is an essential element of life in any society. In the
western capitalistic societies where many of you probably live,
the discussions around work generally focus on what we call
'economic work'. Economic work or paid labour is work that is
carried out (generally) outside of the home for material rewards.
While it is usually not stated so blatantly, these definitions carry
with them an assumed position that paid work is somehow real
work compared to unpaid work. That a person is successful if
and only if they achieve material rewards from their work.

These assumptions inform the arguments around the gender
pay gap and the well-meaning though misguided attempts
to promote women's statuses in society through encouraging

participation in the world of economic work. These harmful views tell women and men that they are 'less than' simply because they choose to work as a parent or carer or do other unpaid work. That they are failures because they work in non-prestigious fields. The mistake the proponents of these views make is that they mistake the end of work for work itself. This mistake is apparent when we hear them talk about the dignity of work, the value of a career, etc.

Purpose of Work

Work's value is predicated only by one thing, its contribution to the achievement of the Purpose. Work of all kinds is always only a means to an end, not an end itself. Work's value is judged by its contribution to the achievement of the Purpose, not by its economic utility, its prestige, or any other feature. In this way, we can genuinely say that the job of being a parent is as important as that of the prime minister, president, doctor, or any other job you may do.

Parenthood is as valuable as any of these more prestigious roles due to the unique nature of parenting, which is inseparable from the Individual Purpose achievement. When you work as a parent, you are directly contributing to the accomplishment of your IP through the education, protection, and guidance of your children. However, this is not to devalue economic work. Unless you are independently wealthy, then economic work is an absolute necessity if you are to survive, let alone achieve your IP. We who aim for our families' and communities' welfare should seek to refocus the discussion on work to focus more on the outcomes for the community and its constituent families compared to its purely economic outcomes.

In this way, we as a society would recognise and value non-economic work in the same way as we value economic work based on its outcome on our collective welfare. We could, by recognising the value all work, celebrate and ennoble parents' and caregivers' vital roles just as we do to doctors and business leaders. Re-dignifying the role of a parent would be to all of our advantages and end the social stigma many full-time parents and carers face.

Focus on Excellence

No matter the type of work an individual chooses to do, the pursuit of the Purpose requires them to maintain their focus on excellence. This is because, as all work is aimed at facilitating the IP, it is valuable and purposeful in itself. There are more desirable jobs, and there are less desirable jobs. There are jobs that contribute more to the welfare of society and jobs that contribute less. However, in their essence, they serve to facilitate the achievement of the Individual Purpose and provide benefit to the community.

If you are a cleaner or a rubbish collector, does your work not have value? Does the income you earn not provide for your family's welfare? Does the service you provide not assist those in your community to achieve their IPs? Of course, it does. This makes it valuable and important and hence worth doing well. It is by recognising the value of all work from the most important to the least glamourous task that requires us to seek excellence in everything we do.

If you build houses, seek ways to do the work better, quicker, cheaper, or to a higher quality. If you are a manager, seek ways to help your team do their work better, seek out and implement ideas to enhance your workers' productivity and welfare. If you are a doctor, seek new methods to protect your patients' health or encourage them to adopt healthier habits. Recognise the power you possess to influence positive change.

Imagine how quickly the world would improve if we all asked ourselves how we could make things better every day in our small spheres of influence. What if we were all focused on the pursuit of excellence in every way? What if every parent was looking for ways to help their children be better? What if every employee was focused on how to be more productive and simultaneously make work more enjoyable? What if every employer cared about their team's welfare and was always looking to help their people enhance their productivity and enjoy their work more? Do you not think that this world would be a happier, richer, and more productive one?

Just think of those people you have worked with that love their work. Are they not happier and more productive than their disengaged co-workers? Is it not they who seem to always come up with the ideas that make the work easier? I warrant that it is the sense of purpose that these people get from their work that propels them forward. It is their realisation that their work matters that differentiates them from the unhappy mass of workers. Fortunately, this happiness is within reach of us all. Just as soon as we recognise the truth that our work, whatever that may be, is infused with value through its contribution to the achievement of our IP, we too can join those happy few for who work is an enjoyable part of life, not a struggle to get through.

This is not to suggest that we should settle for any job—quite the opposite. Just as we should recognise each job's importance and value and pursue excellence in each task, so too should we seek excellence in ourselves. Each one of us has much to contribute. Each one of us can do more than we are. Give 100% where you are, make the work better, but also work on yourself. Self-improvement is an integral part of your work as a person.

Self-Improvement

Self-improvement is not merely a catchphrase. It is imperative for each of us. To ensure the achievement of our Individual Purpose is a constant task. It is not enough to do the minimum, we should be striving to do better, to know more, improve everything, including ourselves. If you are a doctor, then be a great doctor, become a specialist, learn the violin, learn to surf. Whatever you do, don't just settle for what you are, seek to be more every day. If you are a cleaner, then be a great cleaner. If you have the ability and desire to do more, then, pursue that. There is no shame in any work, only in not seeking excellence.

These proposals indicate the type of community that is likely to best support its members in achieving their Individual Purpose. It is now time to move again from the general to the specific. In the next book, we will finish our discussion with a series of short daily exercises, which will help us implement the lessons we have learned if pursued.

VI

Practice

28

Daily Practice

"I am of certain convinced that the greatest heroes are those who do their duty in the daily grind of domestic affairs whilst the world whirls as a maddening dreidel."

Florence Nightingale

On starting your day remember that each day is precious. None of us knows when we will die or what disasters may strike us. We know on waking only that for this day alone, we are alive able to act in such a way as to benefit our families and our communities. Therefore, start each day as recommended by the Stoics bring to your mind the realisation that 'today you may die or be ruined and that what matters is if you live today well or not'. Try to make this a habit each and every morning. Take a moment to think of where you failed the day before and how you can do better today.

Remember that death is inevitable, and for all, we know final and eternal, this life is all we have, and our families' welfare is all that matters. Keep this always before you and when you find yourself tempted to waste time excessively on games or entertainments remind yourself of the shortness of the longest life and how even tomorrow is not promised to us. Remind yourself of the virtues which you aim for and how you can practice them.

As you go about your day, keep the Purpose to which you strive before you. Remind yourself how your work provides for your children, or how you contribute to your community's welfare. Ask yourself, does this act help or harm my family or community. Keep your honour in mind and seek to exercises the virtues.

When things don't go as you had hoped (as they will) remind yourself of all the other things which could have gone wrong and didn't. It is a natural part of the human psyche to notice those occurrences which are unfortunate or unpleasant and yet fail to observe the more dire events which do not happen, yet which could have.

Did your work go poorly today? Remind yourself that you are alive and could not have been. Remind yourself that your car started so you could get to work, that you did not have a car accident on the way to work. That you have a job and are not unemployed, that you enjoy peace when you could be afflicted by war.

Did you fight with your partner? Remind yourself that you

and they are alive when you and they could be dead. Remind yourself that you had the good fortune of finding a partner in the first place when you could be alone. Remind yourself of the virtues which they have, which they could not have had or the vices which they do not have which they could have had.

Are you sick? Remind yourself that you are alive still when you could have been dead. Remind yourself that you were healthy when you could have been ill. That you could have had something worse than you have.

Has a loved one died? Remind yourself that they could have died earlier, that they could have suffered more. Remind yourself that as great as their loss is it could have been greater, or sooner or at a worse time.

In short, seek to bring to mind whenever you are disturbed by the appearance of misfortune that it is generally not as bad as it could have been, that the misfortune could have been greater. That the time you enjoyed the favour of fortune could have been less. This world is governed by random chance or for the more romantically inclined the caprice of fortune. Try as we will we are but at the mercy of chance.

Try to do as Epictetus suggests in the Enchiridion 'Never say of Anything "I have lost it"; but instead say, I had it. Have you lost a job? Do not say I have lost it say instead that you had it and think of how fortunate you were to have it for so long. Your health is going do not say you have lost it instead focus on how long you had it for. The key is to recognise that as when you flip a coin heads or tails equally may appear. So, in life, every moment, fortune can go well or ill. Be happy when things go your way and remember that they could just as easily have gone otherwise.

At the end of the day, devote a few moments to reflecting on the day. Remind yourself that this could have been your last day, and you do not know what tomorrow may bring. Reflect on your successes and failures and determine how you could have done better. A good mantra which I use is a variation of the morning projection.

Each night before I go to sleep, I say to myself "tonight I may die, tomorrow I might be ruined. What matters is that I lived today well". I then ask myself "did I live well today? Where did I do well and where did I fail?" This evening reflection takes just a few moments. But I find it to be invaluable in keeping my focus on the Purpose and in clearing my mind before sleep. Experiment with what works for you. Some people find that keeping a Journal of these reflections can help to keep them accountable. In the end, it doesn't really matter what words or process you use just so long as you take that moment to reflect on your day seeking to see where you acted virtuously and where you could have done better.

If you do these things and if you embrace your true Purpose you will discover as I did that not only will you gain the peace which comes with surety the knowledge of what is right and wrong, the possession of Purpose and the confidence which comes when you are sure of acting correctly. You will discover that the long sort but often transient thing we call happiness will make its self at home. The truth about happiness is simply this 'happiness is not something which can be found it is a by-product of a life lived well and in accordance with virtue and what is right'.

It is my hope that this work will prove enlightening or at least useful to you in your search for the truth. In any rate, I wish you and everyone who reads this work the best fortune in their search. If you found this book helpful share it with those, who may benefit as well. If you believe I erred feel free to reach out to me and offer your critique. Life is a journey, and it is up to each one of us to chart our own path. Use your wisdom and intellect to seek for yourself the truth and always remember as George Herbert is credited as saying 'aim for the moon for even if you miss you may land amongst the stars'. Therefore, do you best always and if you fail, pick yourself up and try again.

About the Author

Andrew Stadtmauer is a Western Australian Folk Philosopher. He seeks through his books to untangle the Purpose of life and how we should live to achieve our Purpose.

You can connect with me on:
🌐 https://www.andrew-stadtmauer.com

Subscribe to my newsletter:
✉ http://bit.ly/3jo88Zq

www.ingramcontent.com/pod-product-compliance
Lightning Source LLC
Chambersburg PA
CBHW051724040426
42447CB00008B/964